"Doing good can take its toll on our lives if we aren't careful. *The Spiritual Danger of Doing Good* is an honest look at the dangers we all need to avoid as we seek to make a difference."

—Craig Groeschel
senior pastor, LifeChurch.tv

"Peter Greer is a friend and a brother, a sparring partner on capitalism and things that matter. As well as anyone I know, Peter lives out the old saying of Jesus: 'Be shrewd as a serpent and innocent as a dove.' This is his newest book . . . full of shrewdness and full of innocence. It is a brilliant reminder that what we do is not nearly as important as who we are—and how much we give is not nearly as important as how much love is in the giving."

—Shane Claiborne
author, activist, and lover of Jesus
thesimpleway.org

"This book is a needed message for all leaders interested in social justice, ministry, or simply loving their neighbors as themselves. It is timely and welcomed. So get ready for a challenge. Peter is a thought leader who is changing the world. Read this book!"

—Brad Lomenick
president and lead visionary, Catalyst

"If you are looking for another fluffy 'how to be a better you' book then keep looking, but if you're ready to take an honest look at your leadership then read this work with a continual prayer on your lips: 'Lord, show me how this might be true in my life.' Too often Christian leaders gloss over these issues at their own peril. Read it, take heed, and become liberated from the hero who must die in order to live—you."

—Dr. Scott C. Todd
senior vice president, Compassion International

"In this extremely timely and important book, Peter Greer applies the apostle Paul's teaching to the twenty-first century leader. Readable, humorous, and keenly insightful."

—Brian Fikkert
author of *When Helping Hurts*

"Anchored in personal, gut-honest experience, *The Spiritual Danger of Doing Good* is a clarion call to all of us. Peter and Anna discuss how to change the world without sacrificing what is most important. I deeply resonate with the principles found in this book. I am taking an inventory of my own journey as a result."

—Stephan Bauman
president and CEO, World Relief

"Peter has nailed it. He has uncovered unique signs and situations we overlook as leaders that cause serious harm to ourselves and to others—particularly those we love most. Want to be a great leader? This is a must read."

—David Spickard
president and CEO, Jobs for Life

"My thought as I was reading was *It's time for us to get off our soapboxes and get off the platforms, roll up our sleeves, and go to work for Jesus and Him alone.* Peter helps us in practical ways to serve Jesus with a pure heart, pure love and, . . . no applause necessary. I believe this book will get you in your gut and you'll be forever changed."

—Anne Beiler
founder of Auntie Anne's, Inc.

"This book will speak truth into hearts that are open. From gorillas in Rwanda to prophets in Panera Bread, the authentic stories and relevant topics will help those in ministry avoid the dangers that so often accompany *doing good*."

—Scooter Haase
executive director, Water Street Mission

"Peter is a veteran leader who shares his experience in a powerful way. This book is for those advocates who live and serve with their neighbors. Peter is well aware of the dangers of service and shares them in a helpful way. This book will help you rediscover the foundations of service."

—Leroy Barber
president, Mission Year

"Insightful, engaging, and eminently readable, *The Spiritual Danger of Doing Good* will pique the hearts, minds, and consciences of anyone who wants to exchange the perils of doing good for the gratitude and security of remembering why we serve."

—Kim S. Phipps, PhD
president, Messiah College
past chair, Council of Christian Colleges and
Universities Board of Directors

"If you hope to better the world, you had better read this book. With striking vulnerability, Peter Greer interweaves his own experiences with biblical truth to expose the dark side of doing good. As a professional 'do-gooder' in a city of do-gooders, I'm buying this book in bulk."

—The Rev. Thomas R. Hinson III
rector, Church of the Advent, Washington D.C.

"I've taken enough photographs to realize there's a greater story behind the image. Peter is willing to take us beyond the portrait of a nonprofit leader to give us a glimpse of the hidden dark side that comes with doing good. This book is honest and a needed challenge for anyone who wants to help change the world."

—Jeremy Cowart
entertainment/humanitarian photographer
founder, Help-Portrait

"YES! Finally. A book, or story rather, about REAL leadership for those who are 'leaders in ministry.' This book is solid gold because of the humility of the author and his desire for all of us to be whole so we can truly serve others."

—Jeremie Kubicek
founder, GiANT Impact

"*The Spiritual Danger of Doing Good* is a forensic exploration of souls in the center of the serving experience. Peter Greer gives us language on how to be mindful of our internal dynamics while we are externally experiencing our faith. *Every* Christ-follower should make this book their surgeon before serving."

—Charley Scandlyn
campus pastor, Menlo Park Presbyterian Church

"In story after story, in a vulnerable and transparent way, Peter shares the truth about doing good. He confesses to identifying with the older son in the parable of the Prodigal Son and to his own pride in his works. Yet he reminds us of the Good News of the grace and love of God—which are unlimited."

—Greg Campbell
former executive vice president,
Coldwell Banker Corporation

"Peter's stature as a Christian nonprofit leader makes his raw honesty about the struggles of service all the more compelling. By sharing how he has persevered through trials in marriage, friendship, leadership, and more, Peter has given us a book that will reach readers in all walks of life. I hope this book finds a home on individuals' nightstands and in group studies alike."

—Tyler Wigg-Stevenson
author, *The World Is Not Ours to Save*
and founder, Two Futures Project

"My brother Peter and I have journeyed together, and I echo with Peter that it's not just what we do, but who we become that is most important. *The Spiritual Danger of Doing Good* is a needed message for anyone eager to follow God's calling for a lifetime of faithful service."

—Carlos Pimentel Sanchez
president, Esperanza International

"I wish I could have read *The Spiritual Danger of Doing Good* as a young pastor. My idealism has often been my greatest strength and my most catastrophic weakness. Peter understands this, and his stories and insights would have saved me from heartache and major mistakes. It is a must read."

—Chris Seay
pastor, Ecclesia Houston

"So often we measure our Christian life by *what* we are doing for God and not *who* we are becoming. We all want heart transformation but often settle for behavior modification. This is a book about the heart. If you choose to read it your heart will never be the same."

—Justin Davis
co-author, *Beyond Ordinary: When a Good
Marriage Just Isn't Good Enough*
co-founder, RefineUs Ministries

"This book is an uncomfortable yet life-giving exploration into the souls of those who desire to bring good to our world. It is refreshingly honest, thoroughly practical, and full of hope for those who are courageous enough to acknowledge their own frailty and need for God's grace."

—Charles Lee
CEO, Ideation and author, *Good Idea. Now What?*

"Peter Greer invites us to see the mighty and redemptive hand of God at work in the midst of weakness. This book not only will challenge you to examine the true motives of your own heart and actions, it will also give you a profound hope to approach and engage in service from the depths of who you are on the inside—one who is daily being formed to be more and more like Christ."

—Bethany Hoang
director, IJM Institute for Biblical Justice

THE SPIRITUAL
DANGER
OF DOING
GOOD

THE SPIRITUAL
DANGER
OF DOING
GOOD

PETER GREER
WITH ANNA HAGGARD

BETHANYHOUSE
a division of Baker Publishing Group
Minneapolis, Minnesota

© 2013 by Peter Greer

Published by Bethany House Publishers
11400 Hampshire Avenue South
Bloomington, Minnesota 55438
www.bethanyhouse.com

Bethany House Publishers is a division of
Baker Publishing Group, Grand Rapids, Michigan

Printed in the United States of America

Library of Congress Cataloging-in-Publication Data

Greer, Peter
    The spiritual danger of doing good / Peter Greer, with Anna Haggard.
        pages cm
    Includes bibliographical references.
    Summary: "Influential social justice leader and President of HOPE International reveals how 'doing good' can be spiritually disastrous for Christians—and how to prevent service from leading to pride, disillusionment, burnout, failed relationships, or loss of faith"—Provided by publisher.
    ISBN 978-0-7642-1102-7 (cloth : alk. paper)
    ISBN 978-0-7642-1156-0 (international trade paper : alk. paper)
    1. Service (Theology) I. Title.
BT738.4.G68 2013
253'.2—dc23   2013008904

Unless otherwise indicated, Scripture quotations are from the Holy Bible, New International Version®. NIV®. Copyright © 1973, 1978, 1984, 2011 by Biblica, Inc.™ Used by permission of Zondervan. All rights reserved worldwide. www.zondervan.com

Scripture quotations identified ESV are from The Holy Bible, English Standard Version® (ESV®), copyright © 2001 by Crossway, a publishing ministry of Good News Publishers. Used by permission. All rights reserved. ESV Text Edition: 2007

Scripture quotations identified GW are from GOD'S WORD®. © 1995 God's Word to the Nations. Used by permission of Baker Publishing Group.

Scripture quotations identified The Message are from The Message by Eugene H. Peterson, copyright © 1993, 1994, 1995, 2000, 2001, 2002. Used by permission of NavPress Publishing Group. All rights reserved.

Scripture quotations identified NASB are from the New American Standard Bible®, copyright © 1960, 1962, 1963, 1968, 1971,

1972, 1973, 1975, 1977, 1995 by The Lockman Foundation. Used by permission.

Scripture quotations identified NIV 1984 are from the HOLY BIBLE, NEW INTERNATIONAL VERSION®. Copyright © 1973, 1978, 1984 Biblica. Used by permission of Zondervan. All rights reserved.

Scripture quotations identified NLT are from the Holy Bible, New Living Translation, copyright © 1996, 2004, 2007 by Tyndale House Foundation. Used by permission of Tyndale House Publishers, Inc., Carol Stream, Illinois 60188. All rights reserved.

Scripture quotations identified NRSV are from the New Revised Standard Version of the Bible, copyright © 1989, by the Division of Christian Education of the National Council of the Churches of Christ in the United States of America. Used by permission. All rights reserved.

Cover design by Faceout Studio

Author is represented by Wolgemuth & Associates.

13 14 15 16 17 18 19   7 6 5 4 3 2 1

To Keith, Liliana, and Myles
May you know how much you are loved.

CONTENTS

FOREWORD

The apostle Paul was clearly the most important leader in the early church. The author of much of the New Testament and the first missionary, Paul launched the most important global movement in all of history. Yet, in the midst of all of this success, Paul said, "So I find this law at work: Although I want to do good, evil is right there with me."[1]

Like all Christians, Paul carried around two natures everywhere he went: his new nature, which was already seated "with [Christ] in the heavenly realms,"[2] and his old nature, which is "hostile to God."[3] Paul explains that these two natures are at war with each other, so that we do not always do the good that our new natures desire to do.[4]

In this extremely timely and important book, Peter Greer applies Paul's teaching to the twenty-first century leader. Readable, humorous, and keenly insightful, this book belongs in the briefcase of every leader every day.

The book opens with the very disturbing finding that only one out of three leaders in the Bible "maintained a dynamic faith that enabled them to avoid abusing their power or doing something harmful to themselves or others. *Only one in three finished well.*" Peter longs for contemporary leaders to have a better track record than our biblical predecessors. Toward that end, he describes the perils and pitfalls that he and other leaders have faced, including neglecting family, moral lapses, pride, worshiping work, false success, spiritual blindness, burnout, and the best one of all . . . "Christian karma."

Peter knows his subject matter extremely well. As the CEO of Hope International, Peter has rightly been lauded as one of the premier Christian leaders in the fight against global poverty. Yet, as Peter very transparently reveals in this book, when he wants to do good, evil is right there with him.

I am finding this book to be immensely practical. Peter uses a host of contemporary examples to bring biblical concepts to life, and the book is full of helpful tips. There are probing questions at the end of each chapter to help you apply the material to your own life. I have personally been very convicted by this book, and I am seeking to implement its wise counsel. In fact, I am planning to use this book in our family devotions, both to get my family's feedback about me and also to better equip our family for faithful Christian service.

Although the book is full of practical suggestions, its greatest strength lies in Peter's awareness that ultimately we cannot gain victory over our old natures by trying harder or following certain techniques. Rather, like the apostle Paul, we must cry out, "What a wretched man I am! Who will rescue me from this body that is subject to death? Thanks be to God, who delivers me through Jesus Christ our Lord!"[5] And as we cry this out every day, we can then rest, not in the good works that we are doing, but in the good work that He has already done.

Brian Fikkert
author, *When Helping Hurts*

INTRODUCTION

A movement of doing good has begun. We sign petitions. We wear the T-shirts. We attend conferences. We volunteer. We give. We go.

People are putting their faith into action by responding to local and global needs with renewed passion and radical commitment. I want to do everything possible to fan this flame and encourage even more outrageous acts of service.

But doing good has a dark side, one rarely acknowledged.

For several years, discussion has centered on charity and its effects on recipients. Does it hurt or help? Economists and authors have recognized that charity can be toxic; our help can actually harm those we seek to serve.[1]

Largely missing from the discussion, however, is the damage that doing good can do to you and me.

For virtually my entire life, I have been actively involved in ministry and have had the privilege of attending great churches, being on prayer teams, participating in mission trips, volunteering locally and abroad, and working full time in international missions and development. And I've noticed something alarming.

While charity can harm others, doing good can also wreak havoc on us.

I have seen friends and mentors throw themselves into the causes of justice and do extraordinary work for Jesus. I admired their passion, their devotion, and their sacrifice. But despite their extraordinary dedication, things went wrong. Burnout. Infidelity. Lost faith. Financial compromise. Personal meltdowns. My heart breaks for these friends and for the ministries they worked so hard to build.

But then I looked at my own life. Even at the pinnacle of my good work, serving refugees in Congo, internally I was at my lowest. I was in a rut of giving and desperately needed to discover a new way of doing good.

When I looked to Scripture for guidance, what I found troubled me. Men and women who had heard from God—who even performed amazing miracles—were just as likely to blow it as everyone else. A study by Fuller Seminary professor Dr. J. Robert Clinton found that only one out of three biblical leaders maintained a dynamic faith that enabled them to avoid abusing their power or doing something harmful to themselves or others. *Only one in three finished well.*[2]

What if the greatest threat to our churches and ministries and spiritual growth is not found in external pressures but within us? Proverbs says, "Above all else, guard your heart, for it is the wellspring of life."[3] Everything flows from the heart—our motivations, our desires, and our *good deeds.* Without evaluating our motives, it is possible to love our service more than we love our Savior. It is easy to pursue working to see "thy Kingdom come" without having a vision of our King. It is possible to be so proud of all we're doing for God that pride chokes our good deeds.

In my zeal for justice and mercy, I made service—a good thing—into the ultimate thing, opening myself to pride, doubt, and approval seeking. My heart unguarded, I found myself vulnerable to the spiritual dangers of doing good. And I'm afraid I'm not alone. The church today is zealous, and we are doing great things. But my concern is that in *doing* great things for God, we will forget who we are *becoming*. Without a clear understanding of *why* we serve, we risk a backlash of relational ruin, spiritual disillusionment, and personal burnout.

Please don't misunderstand me: I truly celebrate the renewed movement of service and am cheering as the church tackles the world's greatest challenges in the name of Christ. But I desperately want more than one out of three of us to finish well. If we are going to finish well, we first need to learn to live well. And to live well, we must ask ourselves: *Why do we serve?* To unearth the answer to this question may help us rediscover the true heart of service.

This book is for anyone loving, giving, and serving. Whether you serve in international ministry or your local soup kitchen, a megachurch or a home church, a community center or your neighborhood, you are part of a great story of hope, and I earnestly desire for you to live a full life of faithful service. But for all of us who serve, we must diagnose and then disarm the spiritual dangers of doing good.

May we learn to love God and serve well.

1

CONFESSIONS OF A DO-GOODER

It might be good theater, but the God who made you won't be applauding. When you do something for someone else, don't call attention to yourself. You've seen them in action, I'm sure—"playactors" I call them—treating prayer meeting and street corner alike as a stage, acting compassionate as long as someone is watching, playing to the crowds. They get applause, true, but that's all they get. When you help someone out, don't think about how it looks. Just do it—quietly and unobtrusively. That is the way your God, who conceived you in love, working behind the scenes, helps you out.[1]

—Jesus

They carried everything they owned on their heads: old milk crates, soggy mattresses, pots and pans. All their worldly possessions amounted to what looked like throw-away items.

Flowing to the rhythm of the rain, the people of Goma poured down red streets. Barefoot or in flip-flops, they streamed down the road to Gisenyi.

Behind them Mount Nyiragongo loomed. Lava oozed from the gash in its crater lake, swallowing entire homes in its path. Leaking through the center of Goma, the volcano forced a migration to the border of Rwanda.

Sitting in a white Land Cruiser, my wife, Laurel, and I watched refugees stream from the Democratic Republic of Congo (Congo) to the border. Just one of a few vehicles on the street, we could not move. People swarmed around our Land Cruiser, peering into it, making us feel even whiter and more out of place than normal. I turned the radio up, but the reggae beats of Lucky Dube, the African Bob Marley, provided no escape.

Most of all, though, I was tired of myself, having caught a glimpse of my true motives.

Though momentarily stuck, I knew we'd leave soon. The crowd would clear. Driving away in an air-conditioned vehicle, I'd watch 400,000 people caught in this catastrophe in my rearview mirror.

They were the ones who were trapped. They had no real option for escape. And when they did return, a "normal life" meant living in extreme poverty, in shacks that seemed unsuitable for a family to call home.

My boss had wanted me to stay another week. I wanted out.

Whether I extended my stay a few days or not, I'd go—return to my job as managing director of a microfinance institution in Kigali, the capital of Rwanda. Unlike the refugees, I could escape this gritty reality.

When I had set out to serve in the refugee camp, I was eager to help and excited about the possibility of making a difference. But the problems were overwhelming. Refugees kept pouring in to the camps. Laurel seemed to cope better than I did, playing hand games and giving hugs to a burgeoning group of children.

I longed for Kigali. The rain never let up. I was weary, tired of wet clothes and sleeping on the floor. Exhausted from never-ending meetings with relief agencies, I was wearier of the politics pervasive among the aid organizations.

Most of all, though, I was tired of myself, having caught a glimpse of my true motives.

Power Play

When we arrived, the United Nations and powerhouse players in global relief assembled in Goma. With a flurry of media coverage, these organizations flew into action. To my surprise, the first "action" was to plaster bumper stickers in the refugee camps. Tacking logos on telephone poles and cars, the nongovernmental agencies (NGOs) marketed their image with New York ad agency efficiency. But somehow, it seemed, they forgot about the people.

Consider the blankets.

Even though we were in central Africa, the rainy season and elevation caused the weather to be surprisingly cold. People living in poverty—who were forced to leave their homes—needed warmer clothes. Between the unrelenting rain and constant chill, I was uncomfortable in my raincoat, long-sleeve shirt, and khakis. A lot of kids wore nothing but ripped t-shirts. And we had blankets to give—generously funded by churches in the U.S. and purchased locally. But we were unable to give them away.

The high-profile NGOs decided how and to whom goods and services were to be provided. Supposedly an American news crew would be following the story of a bundle of blankets arriving in Goma from the U.S. Each NGO wanted the spotlight; the leaders began debating who would give the blankets while being filmed.

Blankets were piled in our van, ready to go. Yet the refugees went without blankets for two days. Until the next shipment arrived, no blankets would be given.

When the delivery finally came, there was no CNN news crew. It had been a rumor.

Because we were no longer competing for media coverage, the larger NGOs finally granted permission for us to distribute the blankets. Even then, it felt like we were under the control of the mafia. As we prepared to hand out blankets, our partner organization herded a few Congolese with the "right look"—those with torn clothes and emaciated faces—to elicit a compassionate response from foreign supporters.

To capture the perfect pictures, they made the Congolese repeatedly walk back and forth as we handed blankets to them.

It felt manipulative and phony. Organizations need to promote their causes and raise support, but why can't they do so in ways that uphold the dignity of the people they serve? The aid industry seemed broken, but it wasn't long before I recognized these same traits within my own heart.

The part of this story that still causes my stomach to churn is when I was finally allowed to distribute the blankets. This was my chance to be in the spotlight. Up on a platform, I bestowed my blankets on people who orderly shuffled through a line. The orchestration was almost perfect—we had roped off lines like at an amusement park—and I was the main attraction.

We had lists of the families so each family received their allotment. Here I was, on the front lines, personally handing out blankets and helping families that had lost almost everything. Noble cause. Noble mission. Noble actions of a twenty-five-year-old relief worker. A photographer snapped pictures, and I smiled wide for the camera as I did "God's work."

And the thought running through my head was not about the people receiving the blankets.

I thought, *I can't wait until the people back home see these photos of me.*

When I saw the photos a few weeks later, I trashed them. With a flaky smile plastered on my face, I could only see the photos as incriminating evidence of an unhealthy heart condition. Captured on film, I recognized myself as playacting for people far away, not thinking about loving the people in front of me.

My friend who took the picture emailed it to me with the caption "cheese." That's exactly how I felt—like artificial Cheez Whiz.

Although I never would have verbalized this, I had wanted to be seen as the good guy, the person my parents could brag about

> **I recognized myself as playacting for people far away, not thinking about loving the people in front of me.**

to their friends, the do-gooder, a masculine Mother Teresa who served the poor. All my life I thought I had been on the right road; I had maintained a clean record and was the "good pastor's kid." But there was a disconnect between my heart and my outward appearance. And I didn't want to talk about it.

Doing good turns out to be a lot more difficult than I originally thought it should be, both in designing programs that really make a positive impact, as well as serving with the right attitude and motivation.

Perhaps that is why, while sitting in the white Land Cruiser that last day in the refugee camp just a week after handing out blankets, surrounded by a surging river of refugees, I just wanted out.

Reprieve

I eventually took a break from Africa by returning to graduate school. For me and countless other young and tired humanitarian workers, graduate school is a socially acceptable way to leave the developing world.

Living near the Arlington/Cambridge town line in Massachusetts, I would ride my 1970 upright Schwinn bike along Massachusetts Avenue each fall morning with my laptop and books strapped on my back, breathing in the cold morning air. I began to feel refreshed. Being away from the messiness of real-life application and plunging into development theory provided an escape. It's so much easier to know the right answers when you're away from people and their situations. And being surrounded by passionate people eager to make a difference in the world was rejuvenating. The time of reprieve passed far too quickly.

A policy analysis exercise was the last major project my fellow students and I needed to complete before graduation. I returned to Congo to investigate how to combine clean water distribution with the work of HOPE International (HOPE).

HOPE, a nonprofit organization, was involved in micro-finance—providing savings, loans, and biblically based business training—to enable the poor to start or expand a business and lift themselves out of poverty. Fascinated by its desire to implement a new program in one of the hardest places on earth to do business, I wanted to get a first-hand look at the ministry before they began to officially operate in Congo.

After a week in Kinshasa, I got an urgent email from my wife to call her immediately. I received the email at 4 a.m. and walked out on the balcony to hear my wife's excited voice say, "Peter, we're pregnant!"

I'm sure I woke the neighbors as we excitedly spoke about all the details—"How did you find out? . . . When is the due date? . . . What names do you like? . . . How will this impact our desire to serve overseas? . . ." I didn't sleep the rest of the night. The hefty phone bill was worth every penny.

The very next day, I had lunch with Eric, the president of the organization, and his wife, Pennie, who happened to be visiting Kinshasa at the exact same time.

While sitting there, he asked me point blank, "Would you consider taking my position in Lancaster, Pennsylvania?" He explained that he was transitioning to another organization, and the ministry was seeking a new president.

My head was spinning. New baby. New job. New place (isn't Lancaster where the Amish live?). Little did I know that "head spinning" would be an apt description of my next stage of life.

Ready, Set, Go

I joined our ministry at just the right time. Not long after my arrival, Muhammad Yunus won the Nobel Peace Prize for his pioneering work in microfinance—unintentionally awakening the North American church to this powerful tool that enables individuals to work their way out of poverty.

Since few faith-based organizations were involved in microfinance, our organization suddenly appeared on the map. With a supportive board, a very generous founder, and a clear vision of where we wanted to go, our ministry grew from its original country of operation, Ukraine, and its presence in China, to launch ministry in the Democratic Republic of Congo.

In short order, we expanded into other underserved parts of the world, including Haiti and Afghanistan. We also partnered with many amazing Christ-centered organizations working all across the globe, including Esperanza in the Dominican Republic and the Center for Community Transformation in the Philippines. Due to an incredible group of dedicated staff members and supporters, we extended our network from serving 3,000 entrepreneurs to over 400,000 in eight years. Fundraising revenue grew tenfold. We celebrated our millionth loan. I wrote a book on microfinance with a friend, had speaking engagements, and traveled extensively.

But slowly, I began to feel the same way I did in that Land Cruiser a few years earlier—tired, disappointed, and as if God wasn't holding up His end of the bargain. If I was doing all this good, where was the peace that passes understanding? Why was my wife emotionally pulling away and creating a life that didn't include me? Why was I dealing with kidnapping, robbery, and murder in the places we operated?

This is not how the Christian life was supposed to work.

At that time, my friend Adrianne sent me an email describing the concept of "Christian karma," and it almost perfectly described my source of discontent. In short, I thought God and I had a deal—what I sow, I reap. What I give, I get in return. When I do good, I get good results.

> *I was on a road leading to continual disillusionment and burnout, no matter where I served or how hard I kept trying to do the right thing.*

But when the returns weren't what I had hoped they would be, I was disappointed. Christian karma wasn't working.

If you've served internationally or in your local church for any length of time, you eventually realize that doing good does not guarantee that only good things happen in your life.

Peering Over the Edge

Looking back, I was on a road leading to continual disillusionment and burnout, no matter where I served or how hard I kept trying to do the right thing.

I needed someone to help me see that I had a warped view of success. That I was becoming isolated and lacked real friends to point out my foolishness. That ministry was becoming more important than faith and family. That my attempts to do good were based on what it did for me and not in joyful response to God's love.

Thankfully, an unlikely man entered my life at exactly the right moment and helped me uncover my faulty foundation for doing good.

Discussion Questions

1. Christian karma is the idea that if you do good, you'll undoubtedly receive blessing. Have you ever bought into this false philosophy?

2. How does a philosophy like Christian karma influence how we serve?

3. When have you served for the approval of others? How do you determine your motives of service?

For photos of the blanket distribution in Congo, see www .peterkgreer.com/danger/chapter1.

SPARKY GRACE

Going through the motions doesn't please you,
    a flawless performance is nothing to you.
I learned God-worship
    when my pride was shattered.[1]

—King David

The first time I met Sparky, I didn't really like him. He didn't care much for me either.

We met at a Christmas party shortly after I had moved to Pennsylvania to serve in ministry. Sitting on an overstuffed couch, Sparky spent the whole evening boasting about his gun collection and talking about the video game Halo 3. I thought his interests did not extend beyond his arsenal of firearms, video games, and overpriced vacations.

Clearly, we have nothing in common, I thought.

When my wife told me that we were going to hang out with Sparky and his wife several weeks later, I was less than excited. But Sparky surprised me. His vocabulary isn't commonly heard in church (*love* isn't the only four-letter word he enjoys), and he has interesting hobbies (recently he had created a homemade grenade launcher), but it didn't take long to realize that he was more genuine in his gritty faith than anyone I'd ever met. Unafraid to ask hard questions, Sparky didn't feel pressure to "act like a Christian." Instead of trying to fit into some culturally influenced G-rated religious play, Sparky was living like someone who had an insatiable hunger to find meaning and purpose.

When he sat down and started sharing his history on our back porch, I felt like I was watching a movie unfold. Growing up in Lancaster County surrounded by well-to-do religious families, Sparky had been the odd one out. From a divorced family, he spent time in bars with his dad on weekends, sipping Coke and cherry juice. Always experimenting, he began using drugs and alcohol at an early age.

Then he met a girl. Carrie convinced him to go back to church. He cleaned up his act. They married. Both career oriented, they landed good jobs. They bought a beautiful white house. They hosted lavish parties. It was fairy-tale perfect.

But happy endings aren't part of Sparky's story. While traveling around the country, Sparky was not only making huge sales, but he was also drinking excessively. The fairy tale ended.

Hitting bottom, he and Carrie started coming back to church. That's when Sparky and I met. The more I learned about Sparky, the more intrigued I became. He was thoroughly unimpressed with religion but seemed desperate to discover if there was something more to life. He pursued truth like no one I'd ever met. Sincere seeking left no room for religious pretense.

Sparky and I couldn't be more different: I'm a pastor's kid; he's a policeman's kid. I grew up eating Jell-O at church potluck suppers, and Sparky grew up in the bar with his dad. I spent my summers on mission trips while Sparky, at ten, was making homemade bombs. Sparky's life was coming apart; I was trying to tiptoe on the straight and narrow.

But sometimes appearances can be wildly deceiving.

A Tale of Two Brothers

Shortly after meeting Sparky, I read *The Prodigal God*, an extraordinary retelling of one of the most well-known parables of all time. This book by Tim Keller did more than just open my eyes to a deeper understanding of one specific biblical story; it started cracking through a superficial veneer of Christian faith.

Contrary to popular opinion, it's not a story about one wayward son—but *two*. Jesus is talking about two brothers, one a hedonist, the other self-righteous. Both are estranged from their father.[2] Therefore, the parable of the Prodigal Son would more appropriately be called the Prodigal Sons.

Typically the parable most of us are familiar with goes something like this . . .

A younger son, defiant and rebellious, demanded his inheritance. His father acquiesced. After squandering everything, the younger son found himself in need when a famine overtook the land. To survive, he took care of pigs, ceremonially unclean animals, even eating their food. Desperate, he returned to his father, intending to be an indentured servant. In an act of extreme generosity, the father welcomed the son and reinstated him as an heir.

It seems pretty straightforward: A wayward son finds grace from a gracious father, an analogy of God's love for us. But Keller says that we miss the point if we leave it at that.

That's clearer when you consider Jesus' audience: the religious leaders and the most upright members of society.

31

In the second, lesser known act of this tale, the elder brother, working out in the fields, heard of his brother returning and the party his father was throwing for him. Disgracing his father, "the older brother stalked off in an angry sulk and refused to join in."[3] In Middle Eastern culture, this is almost as shameful as the younger son's outright defiance. Refusing to participate in one of the greatest parties the father had ever thrown, he dishonored his father.

Again, the father did the unthinkable. Rather than chastising his son, the father demeaned himself by going outside to plead with his son to come in.

> His father came out and tried to talk to him, but he wouldn't listen. The son said, "Look how many years I've stayed here serving you, never giving you one moment of grief, but have you ever thrown a party for me and my friends? Then this son of yours who has thrown away your money on whores shows up and you go all out with a feast!"
>
> His father said, "Son, you don't understand. You're with me all the time, and everything that is mine is yours—but this is a wonderful time, and we had to celebrate. This brother of yours was dead, and he's alive! He was lost, and he's found!"[4]

At the end of the story, despite the same offer of love and forgiveness to both brothers, the elder brother pouted outside while the younger celebrated inside.

Spiritual Dead Ends

Both brothers wanted the same thing: the father's money and possessions. The younger chose to express this through outright defiance, the older through obedience. He believed he gained leverage over his father by doing good.

He felt his father *owed* him.

See how he presented his case to the father: "Look how many years I've stayed here serving you, never giving you one moment of grief." His own work ethic, morality, and service are what kept him from going inside to the party with his father.

It wasn't hedonism that alienated the elder brother from his father; it was all the good things he had done. Good things became ultimate things, creating a barrier between him and his father.

> **It's possible to sacrificially serve God and be completely self-centered in the process.**

The point of the story is that it's possible to sacrificially serve God and be completely self-centered in the process. Morally upright people fully immersed in service can be just as far from God as the young hedonist brother. Eugene Peterson describes it perfectly:

> We've all met a certain type of spiritual person. She's a wonderful person. She loves the Lord. She prays and reads the Bible all the time. But all she thinks about is herself. She's not a selfish person. But she's always at the center of everything she's doing. "How can I witness better? How can I do this better? How can I take care of this person's problem better?" It's me, me, me disguised in a way that is difficult to see because her spiritual talk disarms us.[5]

When reading *The Prodigal God*, my world exploded like one of Sparky's homemade Fourth of July fireworks.

Jesus told this parable to outline two types of people estranged from God: amoral hedonists and the morally righteous. Both paths are spiritual dead ends.

Hedonism and heroism (doing good) are brothers, not polar opposites. Both are focused on ourselves. At their core, both are about wanting our own way. One is wrapped in good deeds and religious service, but both are empty.

This story of the prodigal sons was unfolding in front of my eyes through my relationship with Sparky. He was the younger brother who had returned to the Father, while I was still working hard to earn God's favor. Sparky was interested in a relationship. I wanted a prize—greater recognition and influence. But Sparky understood that the reward *is* the relationship. Frenzied in my constant search to serve, I forgot the point: The gift is God himself. Sparky understood grace and the story of Jesus more than any religious person I'd ever met.

Extravagant Grace

After Sparky hit bottom he came back to a God and a family who showered him with love and forgiveness. He was welcomed to the party, understood grace, and could not contain himself from showering it upon others.

I'm not handy. I'm really not. I recently had a leaky faucet and had to call a plumber because I tried unsuccessfully to make it stop. When the plumber arrived, it took him twenty seconds to turn one loose hose and voilà, no more leaking. I lost eighty dollars and my self-respect as a homeowner.

On the other hand, Sparky is a master craftsman. He was carving wooden birds as a high school student, and he makes elaborate cigar boxes in his free time.

When Laurel and I were away for the weekend Sparky, his wife, Carrie, and another couple decided to surprise us with a home makeover. They must have noticed that Laurel had put up paint swatches and was (subtly) trying to convince me that it was time to paint our dining room.

Somehow Sparky broke into our home, and the foursome didn't just paint the dining room—they transformed our kitchen. They installed crown molding, wainscoting, and quarter round to keep the floor's peeling laminate in place.

When Laurel and I returned from our weekend away, we opened the front door and saw the kitchen illuminated by candlelight. The detail was exquisite and the kitchen felt brand-new.

As Sparky and his team blurted out, "Surprise!" Laurel walked back into the garage and cried.

What made this extravagant giving was that Sparky and Carrie should have been working on their own home. A giant oak tree had recently smashed through their bedroom. Living under a giant blue tarp, they were confined to their family room with plastic sheeting separating the "livable" portion of their home from the disaster zone. Yet they had decided to forget themselves and bless us. We were blown away by their extreme generosity.

> **Younger brothers like Sparky recognize their inadequacies. But they are also overwhelmingly aware that God's love is a gift.**

Sparky didn't need to remodel my kitchen. But it was like he couldn't contain himself from showing others the gift of grace he had received. He was doing it in response to the most incredible love the world has ever known.

Younger brothers like Sparky recognize their inadequacies. But they are also overwhelmingly aware that God's love is a gift. It's not something to be earned. And they're usually the first to join the party.

Philip Yancey once wrote, "The proof of spiritual maturity is not how 'pure' you are but your awareness of your impurity. That very awareness opens the door to grace."[6]

That's Sparky. It's fitting—his last name is Grace.

Discussion Questions

1. Are you more like the younger brother or elder brother in the parable of the Prodigal Sons?

2. How can good things—like success, service, and affluence—keep you from God?

3. Read Luke 15:11–32. What is the father's response to both the elder and younger son in the story? What does the father's reaction suggest about the way God views you and me?

For photos of Sparky and to watch Tim Keller talk about the story of the Prodigal Sons, see www.peterkgreer.com/danger/chapter2.

3

WHEN MINISTRY BECOMES YOUR MISTRESS

The Spiritual Danger of Giving Leftovers to Loved Ones

A [person] ought to live so that everybody knows he is a Christian . . . and most of all, his family ought to know.

—D. L. Moody

A Love Story

"Peter, I met your future wife," my mom abruptly announced to me one summer morning before I returned to college.

Sitting in my parents' kitchen, I looked up, shocked.

"What?" I said. I laughed, but I was surprised. My mom didn't say stuff like that.

The previous week, my mom had taken a group of teens on a trip to Martha's Vineyard in conjunction with Camp Deer Run. Her co-leader was a spunky girl named Laurel. After a week of digging clams, snorkeling, and mentoring junior high students, my mom recognized that Laurel was no ordinary young woman.

A few weeks later, I happened to meet this hazel-eyed woman while I was visiting camp. Introduced to Laurel standing under a gigantic stuffed moose head at the camp lodge, I was intrigued. Clearly, she was smart. She was kind. She was hot.

And she was coming to my college in the fall.

That August I entered my senior year. When Laurel showed up as a freshman, I made sure to make a good impression. Seeing her in the cafeteria with her parents on her first day, I sat with them to help her choose her schedule. And I periodically rearranged my schedule to ensure I could see her between classes.

It wasn't stalking. It was wise planning.

The following summer, Laurel and I worked together at the Christian camp in New Hampshire where she had made such a positive impression on my mother. I quickly discovered that she taught a sign-language class on the lawn outside the chapel every Thursday. So every Thursday I always *happened* to walk by the chapel lawn.

But after camp ended, she was dating someone else.

Soon Laurel was engaged. After a couple years working in Massachusetts, I headed to Cambodia and then Rwanda. We lost contact.

While on a brief trip home from Rwanda for my sister's wedding, I was looking through old family albums, and there was Laurel. It was a picture my mom had taken on the trip to Martha's Vineyard. Laurel was on her tiptoes reaching up to feed a seagull by hand.

Casually I said, "Does anyone know what happened to Laurel?"

I learned she was no longer engaged. (Later I found out that the day she broke her engagement, her brother Paul tried to console her by saying, "Well, you know Peter Greer might still be single.")

My sister also explained that Laurel was trying to find a teaching job in Africa.

I spent the entire flight back to Rwanda crafting the perfect email to Laurel. "Greetings from Africa" was the subject and the email began, "I'm not sure you remember me, but . . ." I tried to make it helpful ("I'll introduce you to all my contacts in Kenya, Uganda, and Rwanda"), witty—and most important, not creepy.

That was the first of a series of correspondence between us. By the time Laurel arrived in Africa eight months later, we had written nearly six hundred emails.

On August 14, I picked Laurel up at the airport in Uganda. We had our first date rafting down the Nile River. Seven weeks later (I didn't want to rush into anything) on my rooftop overlooking Kigali, I proposed. She said yes. A shooting star raced across the sky (seriously).

At the time, Laurel's home in Rwanda didn't have regular running water or electricity. Mine did. I'm still suspicious she married me for my indoor plumbing.

We returned to Virginia for a small family wedding, but also celebrated our marriage with a traditional Rwandan wedding back in Kigali. As is the custom, Laurel disappeared with a group of women for preparations, during which she was clothed in a traditional wedding dress. When she finally emerged at the ceremony, she was led by a group of children singing and dancing, bells jingling around their ankles. Our Rwandan family stood beside us. Our wedding bands have *Ndagukunda* (I love you) written in them.

We honeymooned on the island of Zanzibar off the coast of Tanzania and stayed in a secluded bungalow on the beach. We explored Stone Town, went on spice tours, ate candlelight dinners with waves running under our feet, and even swam with dolphins in the open ocean.

It felt like something from *Out of Africa*. It was perfect.

Then life went very fast. After two more years in Africa, including a short experience responding to the volcano in Congo when we gave away the blankets, we came back to Massachusetts for graduate school. I got a job in ministry. We moved to Pennsylvania. We had our first son, Keith.

As soon as we arrived in Amish Country, USA, we joined one of the largest churches in the area. We plugged in to a small group. Attended church picnics. Hosted Christmas parties. Taught Sunday school. Volunteered with children in the nursery.

Meanwhile, our family kept growing. Our daughter, Liliana, was born. We adopted our son Myles from Rwanda. Laurel and her friends started a nonprofit to provide clean water in Rwanda. Between work, church, family, and friends, our lives were filled to the max.

We were doing a lot of good things . . . and we were drifting apart.

The Crash

Looking back, I see how my overwhelming emphasis on work and heavy travel schedule had caused Laurel to create a life that did not depend on me. She was learning to live without me. Her friends became her support structure. She could not count on me for a consistent family routine, so she created her own. Tensions always rose before and after trips. She didn't want to call out the problems we were having because she believed in what I was doing and wanted to be a supportive spouse. She was willing to put up with a lot, but eventually, she pulled the emergency brake to save our marriage.

"You are choosing your ministry over me—and I feel nothing for you."

One evening after the kids were in bed, Laurel said one of the most frightening sentences I have ever heard: "You are choosing your ministry over me—and I feel nothing for you."

She said she was committed to me, but she had been growing increasingly discontent in our marriage.

I was blindsided by the comment. We had such a good start. We knew that God had brought us together. I loved my wife. I loved my kids. But I was shocked into the realization that somehow my ministry had become my mistress.

The Unexpected Affair

It starts innocently enough.

One day you stay late at work to finish a report. You're being responsible, helping your teammates by pulling your share of the workload.

But there is something appealing about the night.

Staying late, you get results: Your boss likes your work. You get the job done and you do it *well*. You are the company's rising star.

So your one night becomes several. You tell your spouse there's no cause for alarm. It's busy season.

Busy season becomes a busy year. Which turns into two. Then three.

And then things begin to change. Yes, there's always the guilt. And you still have to make that dreaded call saying you won't be home for dinner.

But you feel something else too. At work, you're needed, you feel affirmed—you're indispensable.

At home, you're not. At least not in the same way.

You don't get an excellent performance review for being a supportive spouse, or changing your newborn's diaper, or reading bedtime stories.

For me, I had been away more than a hundred nights a year. Even more of those nights I had come home from work late, not having dinner with my kids. Laurel was virtually operating as a single mom. And I was building a "successful" ministry.

I was so focused on the demands and feelings of worth at work that I missed both the joy and significance of my key role as a husband and father.

If you've felt the demands of both work and family; or if you are single, and you're juggling friends and family (and you can justify staying late at the office because there's no one telling you to come home), then you have experienced how easily work can become your mistress.

Change of Plans

After Laurel's words, I went into crisis mode: I canceled the business trip I was planning to take to Peru. I cleared my work schedule. And I focused on restoring relationships in my family.

But troubleshooting doesn't work at home like it does at the office. There are no quick fixes. I had lost Laurel's trust and partnership and it took time for her to believe that the changes were real.

I had fallen for a dangerous lie in ministry. If *Serving God Through Service = Good* . . . then *Serving God Through More Service = Better.*

If you are running hard for God, overextended, neglecting family and friends for the sake of the ministry, some people will celebrate your dedication. Isn't it good when we give it all in service to others?

But too much of even a good thing can harm you and those around you.

Your mom made you take your vitamins. Without vitamins, your body would develop skeletal defects, eye impairments, dermatitis, anemia—in essence, your body would begin to break down.

But taken in high doses, Vitamins A, D, B_6, and iron are highly toxic.[1] Too much iron in our systems can cause liver failure, low blood pressure, depression, coma, and death. Iron supplements are the number-one cause of death "from accidental overdose" in children, according to a study at Georgetown University Hospital in Washington, D.C.[2]

Similarly, overdosing on service can be particularly toxic.

The Tragedy of Ministry Overdose

Bob Pierce was a young and enthusiastic Christ follower. In 1947, he was serving Youth for Christ in China. Seeing overwhelming poverty, he was moved by compassion.

He decided to act. When he came back to the United States, he had pictures of impoverished Chinese children in hand, those that people could "adopt." And that was the beginning of World Vision, a leading relief and development organization.

The ministry flourished, but his home life didn't. His travel extended up to ten months a year. In 1963, "he had a nervous breakdown." Following his breakdown, he virtually "disappeared" for nine months, traveling around the world while neglecting his family.

Traveling with World Vision in 1968, he received a call from his daughter. She requested that he return home. She said she was in trouble.

He told her he couldn't. He had just resigned from World Vision, and he needed to lengthen his farewell tour.

Soon after, his daughter attempted suicide. And though she didn't succeed on her first attempt, within the year she had taken her life. Pierce checked into rehab in Switzerland for a year after her death.

But the next year, he became the leader of an organization that became known as Samaritan's Purse. Meanwhile he and his wife's relationship grew increasingly strained. In 1970, Pierce and his wife, Lorraine, separated.

The remaining eight years of his life, Pierce was isolated from his family until a beautiful reconciliation the week he died.

When he was still at the peak of his ministry at World Vision, he said, "I've made an agreement with God that I'll take care of his helpless little lambs overseas if he'll take care of mine at home."

My heart breaks for Pierce and his family.

There is no doubt he had a genuine heart for the poor. He penned the famous lines, "Let my heart be broken with the things that break the heart of God." He founded two of the largest Christian ministries in the world.

God used his ministries in incredible ways. But he paid a very high price as his personal life unraveled.[3]

Does this sort of devotion to ministry honor God? Is there another way?

Inside-Out Development

We invited Beth Birmingham to speak at our organization's annual leadership summit this year. Beth—a professor at the School of Leadership and Development (SLD) at Eastern University—is a captivating speaker.

She's also an expert on the dangers of a workaholic approach to ministry.

Looking around at a room of worn-out, high-achieving international development leaders, she said to us, "Transformational leadership begins at home."

No matter what the numbers at work say, we aren't a success unless our children and spouses are on board with what we do.

What does an inside-out approach to ministry look like?

If you're married, recognize you hold a covenant with your spouse, not your work. God ordained the biblical covenant of marriage. He didn't create one for work. Your first priorities are God, the very center of all we do, and then your family. And then—and only then—your work. The problem is that we confuse our service to God with our vocation, and the two are not synonymous.

I do not want to look in my rearview mirror and see a broken family which only got my leftovers. According to statistics compiled by Bill Bright, founder of Campus Crusade for Christ (Cru), "Eighty percent of pastors' spouses feel their spouse is overworked . . . and 50 percent of pastors' marriages will end in divorce."[4]

Billy Nolan, who leads GlobalX, the international ministry of North Point Community Church in Alpharetta, Georgia, developed an unusual recruiting process when screening mission partners. At North Point they not only recruit organizations with leaders who have competence and commitment to ministry. But they also look at the health of the leaders' family lives. They formally interview the individuals' families, recognizing that ministry success is entirely linked to a healthy family and a balanced life.

> *I do not want to look in my rearview mirror and see a broken family which only got my leftovers.*

What if we took that one step further? What if before you accepted a promotion, Human Resources required you and your spouse to sign a document that shows your joint decision to take on additional responsibilities? Together you sign on to your job. Together you identify potential pitfalls of the new job—how it will affect your family and your community. Together you could create a vision for your family/work life.

This is not just an issue for married men and women. If you're single, it's just as easy to become a servant-hearted workaholic. In fact, with fewer boundaries, an unbalanced life could be an even greater threat. Without boundaries, you're equally as likely to miss out on deep relationships with family and friends and become isolated and less effective in your service.[5]

The Vomit of the Religious

Jesus said that in comparison to our love for God, it's as if we "hate" our family. But at the same time, he was adamant that family needs take first priority over religious service.

> Why do you use your rules to play fast and loose with God's commands? God clearly says, "Respect your father and mother," and, "Anyone denouncing father or mother should be killed." But you weasel around that by saying, "Whoever wants to, can say to father and mother, What I owed to you I've given to God."[6]

Jesus was calling out those abusing the oral tradition of "corban."

As a Jew in the first century, you could set aside some of your funds for religious purposes—often for the building of the temple. This was called "corban." It was basically money that was dedicated to God.

But some of the religious leaders were using corban in order to neglect the needs of their parents.[7]

The fifth commandment, to "honor your father and your mother"[8] wasn't merely about respect; it meant caring for the physical needs of your family. More specifically, it meant that you would keep your parents from falling into poverty.[9]

And the religious were intentionally using corban—religious tradition—as a way to forgo using their personal funds to care for their own parents.[10] They claimed that their money was dedicated to God and therefore they did not need to provide for their families.

Jesus condemned them for this: "That can hardly be called respecting a parent. You cancel God's command by your rules. Frauds! . . . Listen, and take this to heart. It's not what you swallow that pollutes your life, but what you vomit up."[11]

What the religious left in their wake—their "vomit"—was fractured families and unhealthy relationships.

Guardrails

Laurel and I have worked together over the past few years rebuilding our marriage. I never want to return to the place we were before when I gave her my leftovers. But like an addict who understands his own vulnerability for another drink, I know my own heart well enough to know how easy it would be to once again steamroll family in the pursuit of doing good.

We began meeting with marriage coaches. But more than anything else, getting back into the habit of praying daily together has turned our relationship right-side up. When you come before the Creator of the Universe with your spouse, suddenly your perspectives change. Your arguments seem smaller. The Beloved draws you together. Everything changes when you invite God in.

Also what has revolutionized our marriage are simple guardrails to better balance work and family. These are not foolproof techniques or the "cure" for the challenges of marriage; they are simply a few things we've done to protect our marriage.

Write My Resignation

To show Laurel that my decision to prioritize my marriage over my work wasn't just a short-term change, but a long-term commitment, I actually handed Laurel my resignation letter. I wrote it, addressed it to the board of directors, and sealed it in an envelope. I told Laurel that if she felt that I was not being the husband and father she needed me to be, she could mail my letter to the chair of our board. And with that, I would officially resign. I would walk away from the ministry where I serve, because I have a higher commitment to Laurel. Never again am I willing to be "successful" at work but a failure at home.

> **What has revolutionized our marriage are simple guardrails to better balance work and family.**

Tuck the iPhone in a Drawer

One day I was helping my two-year-old son get breakfast while reading work email on my iPhone.

He grabbed me by the pant leg and said to me, "No phone, no phone."

It broke my heart. I had such a small amount of time with him and I was missing it. Now, I literally put my phone in the kitchen drawer until my kids go to bed so I know my focus is on my family.

The short time between dinner and bed is precious, and I'm not going to miss it.

Ask!

I monitored key performance indicators on the health and welfare of our programs, yet I rarely asked my wife how she was doing. I did not know she was feeling alone in our marriage.

Periodically now I do "impact assessments"—ten simple questions that help me know how I can better support her.

- Do my actions show you that apart from Jesus Christ, I have no higher love?
- How well are we serving together?
- How well am I encouraging your spiritual growth?
- How well am I guarding our time together?
- How is our prayer life together?
- How well am I supporting you to grow in your gifts/skills?
- Are we discipling our children well together? How convinced are you that parenting is truly a partnership?
- How well am I caring for your friends?
- How is our physical expression of love? (Ahem . . . the language of this question has been edited.)
- What can I do to love you better?

Limit Travel

We receive great opportunities at work. I felt like I had to say yes to all of them. Recently I limited my travel to six nights per month,[12] and we've created a policy at HOPE that no staff member travels more than seventy-five nights a year without authorization from senior leadership. By saying no to good opportunities, I get the chance to tuck my children into bed *and* to say yes to the best ones.

Get Over Yourself

Before the conversation with Laurel, I had an inflated view of my importance. At work, I felt I had to do it all. Besides being wrong, this attitude spread me too thin. I was too frazzled to do anything well.

Invest in Friendships

In addition to the previous suggestions, it's essential to truly invest in deep friendships. We were built for relationships. I have invited a council of close friends to be my accountability partners for the area of work-life balance.

Sometimes it's no fun because they ask me tough questions. And they don't let me off the hook.

Although it doesn't have to be formal, having friends who love you enough to ask you the tough questions makes a huge difference in all areas of life, including how late you stay at the office. Just make sure you find people who will truly (and humbly) confront you when you cross the line.

Beyond Good Intentions

Since the turning point conversation with Laurel, I have decreased many responsibilities, including the number of staff reporting to me, and delegated everything except the most important aspects of my role. It's liberating: I'm now able to focus on the areas in which I excel, and I have more balance than ever before.

The bottom line is this: It doesn't honor God to steamroll over friends and family in pursuit of service. I am so grateful that Laurel had the love—and courage—to confront me about my priorities.

We have so much to lose when we steamroll family in pursuit of doing good.

If ministry begins at home, then let's be intentional. Plan for it. Prepare for it. Don't think that a vibrant family life just happens. And be brave enough to involve our family and friends when considering career aspirations, even if our aspirations are noble ministry pursuits. What happens at home impacts our faith and our service, and we have so much to lose when we steamroll family in pursuit of doing good.

Discussion Questions

1. In an increasingly interconnected world, it's more difficult than ever to find work-life balance. What have you done to create boundaries?

2. Do you find that you are fully present with your family and/or friends or are you often distracted by details of work and other obligations? When are you most likely to be physically present but emotionally distant?

3. What are some guardrails that can help you keep a healthy work-life balance?

4. As Christ-followers, we are called to surrender our lives—
and that means our time—to our Savior. What does that
look like for you?

For photos of Laurel and where we first met, see www.peterk
greer.com/danger/chapter3.

STUCK IN A RUT

The Spiritual Danger of **Doing** Instead of **Being**

I am the vine; you are the branches. If you remain in me and I in you, you will bear much fruit; apart from me you can do nothing.[1]

—Jesus

Right before Laurel and I hit our low point, our ministry was growing rapidly. It seemed as if God was blessing us.

But growth and good works do not guarantee you're heading in the right direction. In fact, Jesus says many service-oriented, creative, talented, religious people will come to Him on Judgment Day and say, "Look at the works we have performed in your name, the miracles, the prophecies."

But Christ will say to them one of the most shocking statements recorded in all Scripture, "I never knew you."[2]

It is possible to be successful, even in service, yet be heading in the wrong direction.

Stuck

After Laurel and I had "the conversation" that changed our marriage, we decided it was probably overdue for our family to escape together for a few days. No cell phone. No email. Just our family and a welcome change of pace.

Greg and Helene, dear friends, were kind enough to let us stay at their home in Outer Banks, North Carolina. We left at 10 p.m. so our kids would sleep on the eight-hour journey. Driving through the night, we not only missed all the traffic winding around Washington, D.C., but we also arrived at the beach just as the sun was beginning to rise. The road literally dead-ended at the beach.

As we turned onto the final stretch of deserted beach, there were wild horses playing amid the crashing waves. It was an incredibly beautiful setting.

Beautiful but rugged. Greg cautioned us that we needed four-wheel drive to make the last nine miles to his home. In the sand, multiple ruts formed by other vehicles went before us. Some led farther down the beach, some led to other homes, but we needed the one that led to our destination: the beach house.

Without giving it much thought, I simply chose a rut and began driving. My thinking was that if it started to send me the wrong way, I could simply redirect, switch to a different pair of tire tracks. However, it wasn't long before I learned something: You go where the rut leads you.

Changing course seemed impossible.

Bouncing along the sand, I realized this is exactly what I had done in my relationship with Laurel and in my relationship with God. I had not chosen my path carefully and was furiously driving in a rut of service, but moving away from a life grounded in grace.

I thought I would be able to fix our marriage with a few days together on a beautiful beach, especially when I had secretly purchased enough of Laurel's favorite things—from chocolates to clothes—to give her a daily gift. I had also packed the emails we wrote to each other when I was in Rwanda and Laurel was living in Washington, D.C. But I discovered that some ruts run deep.

When the road originally dead-ended at the beach, the ruts looked like they all led to the same place, but a slow divergence compounded by miles of sand led to entirely different destinations. It was like our friends who tried to visit us in Carlisle, MA, but ended up in Carlisle, PA. One incorrect letter made a huge difference in destination.

I would not be able to escape the rut I followed for years in a week—I had to do some significant backtracking to discover where I had gotten onto the wrong path.

The backtracking went past specific behaviors that needed to change and led me to the place where lasting change begins: my heart and the very foundation for service.

Road Signs

So how do we know if we are in the wrong rut with our service? Looking back, I see some of the subtle warning signs:

- I had forgotten *why* I was serving.
- My focus was on *what* I was doing instead of *who* I was becoming. Time in prayer and study of Scripture was marginalized and seen as less important than all the *good work* I had to do.
- A pursuit of recognition overshadowed my pursuit to grow closer to Christ.

- "My ministry" was growing and I felt like it must be because of something I was doing right. It was possible to do my job relying on my strength, my creativity, my performance, my gifts, and my talents instead of an utter reliance on God and His power.
- With such a busy schedule, I had no time for relationships and friendships with people who could have helped me spot the slow drift.

We need to remember that Jesus clearly said, "Apart from me you can do nothing."[3] Jesus didn't say *little*. He said *nothing*.

The truth is we can spend our lives giving, serving, and going, but if it is apart from His Spirit, it amounts to a garbage pile of good intentions.

Wall Street or Rwanda

Unless we rediscover the foundation of service, our good works can be all about us: promoting our image, heightening our own vanity and pride. Service becomes a means to achieve our dreams, our purposes, our goals. Phony activism and selfish service will eventually be exposed.

Most assume a Wall Street investment banker would have a bigger ego than a humanitarian aid worker in Africa. But I have been around do-gooders my entire life—and am one—so I know there's a desire to be seen as the hero in all of us.[4]

Christ: Religious Outlaw

Service is radically different when we return to the *why* behind it. In almost every religious system, service is a means to an end. Service becomes the secret to getting things, a pass to the afterlife, blessings, a respectable name—even a way to feel good about ourselves.

Our performance dictates our destiny. If we're Buddhists, we find bliss through self-restraint, following the Noble Eightfold Path. Muslims get to heaven by obeying the Five Pillars of Islam. Even atheists can achieve respectability through good deeds. And many practicing Christians take the same approach: *If we do good, we'll earn favor with God.*

But Jesus Christ defied religion. Upending the cosmic scale that weighs our good and evil, Christ did the unthinkable: "But God demonstrates his own love for us in this: While we were still sinners, Christ died for us."[5]

> **Unless we rediscover the foundation of service, our good works can be all about us.**

The core message of grace is religious anarchy. We are forgiven, accepted, and loved not because of what we do, but because of what Jesus Christ has *already* done on the cross. Independent of our performance, we are loved. We simply can't earn the forgiveness we desperately need, which God freely offers through Christ.

As followers of Jesus, we don't serve because it's a means to an end. It's not a ticket to heaven, a way to have a respectable life, or a way for people to think well of us.

We serve out of overflowing gratitude that we are loved by a God who knows we don't have it all together. We serve in response to the greatest generosity the world has ever known— "For God so loved the world that He *gave* . . ."[6]

Unfortunately, it's our natural inclination to forget about the radical message of grace and just keep trying harder.

Lollipops and Incentives

Grocery shopping with kids is every parent's nightmare. There are just too many temptations for a kid to eat, to knock over, and to whine about.

When I take my kids to the grocery store, I promise a lollipop or some treat for good behavior, an incentive (another word for *bribe*).

As we get older, lollipops are replaced with keys to our parents' car or new clothes if we get good grades. By the time we reach adulthood, we're well trained.

In the workplace, if we make our bosses look good and exceed expected results, we'll get recognition and a raise.

When we bring this performance mentality into our relationship with God, we commit spiritual heresy and miss out on the very center of the message of Jesus.

Faith ≠ Checklist Manifesto

I like checklists. Seriously, few things give me a high like crossing things off my list. I'm such a big fan of them that I made *The Checklist Manifesto* by Atul Gawande mandatory reading for our organization's leadership. It's not a real page-turner, but it's full of ways to create simple, repeatable, and checklist-able activities to deliver a world-class product or service.

I also like checklists with God. I like being able to cross off the box that I went to small group, did my devotionals, said my morning prayers, cared for the poor.

In theory, the concept of grace is attractive. But recognizing that I can never meet the expectations for God—that being good enough is out of reach—is uncomfortable. Realizing I can't *do* anything for God that would make Him accept me more leaves me feeling a bit unsettled. It's harder to keep score and know if we're meeting the core requirements of faith.

If I don't have a religious to-do list—then how am I supposed to know if I've met the minimum requirements?

I'll do whatever you want, God. Just give me a checklist.

But God isn't asking us to follow a checklist: The Almighty wants us to understand and respond to His love. We are *already* forgiven and adopted into His family through the gift of undeserved love beautifully exemplified on an ugly cross.

This is why checklists don't work in our relationship with God. Checklists can curb behaviors but they can't change hearts. Unless we are responding to the God who loved us first, our good works actually become deadly, the antithesis of the Gospel.

The Spiritual Danger of Doing Good

My hope is that this book will detail specific dangers that come with doing good and offer practical suggestions of how to equip you to live, give, serve, and go with greater passion and commitment.

But I'm concerned that I'll simplify the depth of the problem we face and provide superficial answers. Or you'll make a checklist. Checking off what you've done right, and what to avoid, you'll rely on your own creativity, your own merit—on you—to do good.

The prophet Jeremiah wrote, "The heart is deceitful above all things and beyond cure. Who can understand it?"[7] Our ability for self-deception is greater than we realize—and we desperately need a Savior to save us from ourselves.

> *God only uses flawed people who rely on Him.*

So What Now?

If in reading this book, you begin to see how selfishness and pride disfigure your service, remember that being broken doesn't disqualify you. It's the exact opposite. God only uses flawed people who rely on Him. People who recognize that it's about God's Spirit. God's grace. God's power. God's plan.

The starting point to give, serve, and love with more enthusiasm, more focus, and more longevity is the belief that:

- You can waste your life doing good things if they are apart from a deep and intimate relationship with Christ.

- Christ is the Savior and you're not. You can stop pretending it's all up to you and instead start living a life of generous service that is merely a response to the love you've already been shown.

So accept that you're inadequate. Embrace the fact that you're needy. Don't try to prove to God you've earned His favor. Let Jesus Christ flood your life with forgiveness, acceptance, and love.

And then get to work responding to His grace by bringing healing to the hurting, Good News to the poor, hope to the hopeless, and freedom to the oppressed.

There is a remarkable story of grace ready to begin.

Discussion Questions

1. Why do you serve?

2. Have you ever fallen into a performance mentality in your spiritual life?

3. How do you go about checking the condition of your heart?

4. Who has modeled a life of grace to you?

For family photos and to hear Atul Gawande speak about *The Checklist Manifesto*, see www.peterkgreer.com/danger/chapter4.

SILVERBACKS AND SMALL STEPS

The Spiritual Danger of Justifying Minor Moral Lapses for a Good Cause

When giftedness outweighs character, implosion isn't a matter of *if* but of *when*.

—Justin and Trisha Davis

Just before leaving Rwanda, Laurel and I made a final stop to see the true king of the jungle, the elusive mountain gorilla.

After hiking for three hours, we came upon a Susa gorilla family. Fewer than eight hundred of these amazing animals live in the wild, and we were able to spend an hour watching forty of them play in their natural habitat. It was spectacular: The juvenile gorillas wrestled while the mother gorillas cared for the young. The silverback male ate bamboo at a distance and cautiously eyed our group of eight visitors.

I should have known this was inappropriate in *every* culture, but I began photographing a nursing gorilla. The 500-pound silverback suddenly jumped up and without warning ran over to me on all fours, grabbed me by my coat, and began dragging me into the forest.

Laurel screamed, "Peter, NO!" and attempted to run after me, but thankfully was restrained by her friend.

After dragging me ten feet, the gorilla let me go. And just to make sure everyone knew he was king of the jungle, he stood up and beat his chest. There was absolutely no question who won this brief wrestling match.

My friends had given me the Kinyarwanda name *Muzungu Cyane Cyane*, meaning the "whitest of the white man." At that moment, the nickname was very fitting as the guards helped a *very white* man find his camera and get up on his feet.

After realizing I was not injured, I knew this was going to make a good story. And the best part was that the entire episode was captured on camera by a French photographer who was working on a book on primates. Instead of running to my aid, he snapped picture after picture showing the gorilla charging me, grabbing me, and running away. He subsequently sold the pictures and story to *ParisMatch*, a French news and celebrity lifestyle magazine. He described me as an American tourist who didn't know how to behave around gorillas.

Moral Lapse for a Good Cause

Just last week, as our neighbors asked us to tell this story at a Sunday afternoon pool party, I recognized the story had changed. Originally, the gorilla dragged me ten feet. But then it was fifteen. And at the pool party, it was twenty . . .

This story doesn't need any embellishment. And yet, I was exaggerating how far the gorilla took me.

And I haven't exaggerated only the gorilla story.

In speaking to groups, I have added a few more details to

better support the point I'm making. If the beginning of one story fits better with the end of another, does everyone really have to know it's two different stories—especially if it's for a good cause?

No matter how good these stories are, or no matter how much they prompt a good response, it is wrong. And there is no such thing as a minor moral lapse for a good cause.

Solomon writes in Proverbs, "There is a way that appears to be right, but in the end it leads to death."[1]

Especially for those who are doing good, it's easy to justify minor moral lapses as long as the end objective is noble.

When our friends and supporters hear about our service projects, they tend to only want the good news, so we oversell the impact. We pretend there are easy solutions to complex problems. We're rewarded for rhetoric rather than reality. Polish the truth. Simplify the story. Telling the full truth hurts our sales numbers (and doesn't get re-tweeted as often).

As long as it's for a worthy cause, it's not a big deal, right? But it doesn't work that way.

It is like jogging ten minutes and then devouring three king-size Snickers bars. You'd burn 100 calories jogging and then inhale 1500.

The spiritual danger of doing good is to think your service entitles you to make minor moral lapses, whether it's stretching the truth or justifying guilty pleasures. Right after moments of significant service, my heart is most unguarded. Often doing good things makes you believe *I deserve just this little thing because of all of my sacrifices.*

An attitude of entitlement is morally toxic. You begin to believe you're above the system.

Consider founders of organizations. "When you're the founder, you think you can do anything and that the rules don't apply to you," said Mark Cheffers, CEO of AccountingMalpractice .com.[2]

Don't forget it: The rules *do* apply to you.

Small behaviors infect our whole lives, extending to the way we use our credit cards, enjoy entertainment, lust after success, or work at our jobs.

"If their life is a lie, it's not confined to their personal life. If they are lying to their wives, there's huge potential they are also lying to their colleagues, their board of directors, and potentially their auditors," said U.S. Attorney for Maryland Thomas Di Biagio on those who have compromised in the workplace.[3]

> **Don't forget it: The rules *do* apply to you.**

Small compromises are the gateway drug to acts with big consequences. No one simply falls into sin, or suddenly wakes up in bed with his best friend's wife. When you hear of individuals or organizations that have made major ethical compromises, chances are attitudes and decisions have been undermining them for years. If you take enough small steps, you can walk very far from your starting point. And there are huge costs to family and friends. In many cases, when people fall, families are torn apart.

After justifying a few little moral compromises—embellishing a story, misrepresenting funds, not guarding your eyes, turning the other way when you see something questionable—you're more likely to repeat it. Slowly, you'll become anesthetized to sin.

The tallest oak tree began as an acorn—and the biggest moral failure began as a small compromise.

Or a slight exaggeration of a story.

Borrowing Just a Little Bit

When serving as the managing director of a Rwandan microfinance institution, I had my first experience of fraud.

Two weeks after I returned from my honeymoon, a senior employee came into my office on Friday at 4 p.m. Shutting the door behind her, she related how she had witnessed another employee destroying documents. Receiving this tip on a Friday was fortuitous. Over the weekend, I had complete privacy to carry out a full investigation of our office records. My research revealed that eight employees had committed theft.

I considered them all good friends.

On Monday—after documenting my evidence and seeking confidential counsel from my supervisor, a Rwandan lawyer, and the technical support team overseas—I had one of the most heartbreaking days of my life.

When the employees arrived at work at 8 a.m., they were quarantined to keep them from collaborating. An action team consisting of a Rwandan lawyer, two senior staff, and me conducted individual interviews with each of the suspects.

By the end of the day, each of the perpetrators confessed to his or her crimes. Along with their resignation letters,[4] they also signed legally binding agreements to repay the stolen funds.

I broke down in my office, partially because I was forced to say good-bye to friends, but also because I felt as if I was responsible.

In the interviews, it became clear that most of the employees had never *intended* to steal money. Initially, each thought they would just borrow a little. They were good people who loved God. But they had short-term needs—medical emergencies, family members in need of cash. With systems not stringent enough to stop them, they helped themselves to "just a little" with the hope of returning the funds. Unfortunately, this thinking led to a snowball of stealing and they were caught.

Though they looked innocuous, similar small steps led an ancient leader astray.

Leader Charged on Counts of Adultery, Murder

You know the story of David and Bathsheba. It's easy to wonder how a man of God could do so many horrendous things in the span of one chapter.

Where did David go wrong? Most of us may be tempted to skip immediately to where he had Bathsheba brought to his palace. However, by that point, David had already taken multiple small steps in the wrong direction.

David took his first step in the first verse of the chapter: "In the spring, at the time when kings go off to war, David sent Joab out with the king's men and the whole Israelite army. They destroyed the Ammonites and besieged Rabbah. *But David remained in Jerusalem.*"[5]

"The time when kings go off to war." In ancient cultures, it was the duty of the king to go to war with his men. But King David stayed behind in Jerusalem.

No big deal. He had fought countless wars already and won them. If any king ever had the right to skip a battle, it was David. Right?

While David was behind in Jerusalem, he happened to stroll around his roof and see Bathsheba bathing. David then chose to look at her instead of looking away.

He was the king, wasn't he? In surrounding cultures, kings were above the law and did as they pleased. Besides, David had been a righteous man. He had protected the people and led them well. If anyone had the right to look at the people, surely it was he. Wasn't it?

But David found that looking was not enough. He wanted to know about her. He was certainly allowed to find out more information on a citizen. That didn't hurt anyone. So he asked a servant of his who she was. He was informed that her husband, Uriah, was off at war (where David should have been).

David decided to have Bathsheba brought to his palace. Even

at this point, he could have just had an engaging conversation. There's nothing wrong with a conversation, right? Perhaps he could have comforted her while her husband was away. Bringing comfort to a lonely woman is a good thing, right? And maybe he could have just given her a little hug. There's no harm in a little hug, right? And maybe they could have just gone to the bedroom, where they could have had some privacy to talk some more.[6]

It was after all these *little steps* that David stepped into the sin of adultery.

Before we know it, in a cover-up gone wrong, David ended up murdering Uriah, one of his most loyal mighty men.

When we see the end of the story, we are left with our mouths gaping. How could godly David have strayed so far? This story contains dozens of small steps—minor compromises easily justified.

By allowing one little lapse, David opened the door for another, and another, until finally he ended up in a place he never intended to go.

In the Sermon on the Mount, Jesus called us to go beyond the Law to the heart of the issue. Exploring issues like murder, adultery, and divorce, Jesus said our thoughts and attitudes matter. Not only is murder wrong, uncontrolled anger is too. Adultery is sinful, but so are wandering eyes.

> *There are no minor moral lapses. We go from attitudes to thoughts to behaviors in an easy progression.*

And they often lead to death: "For out of the heart come evil thoughts—murder, adultery, sexual immorality, theft, false testimony, slander. *These are what defile a person.*"[7]

There are no minor moral lapses. We go from attitudes to thoughts to behaviors in an easy progression.

I am under no illusion that I am immune to ending up in the same situation as David. If this godly man who had direct interaction with the almighty God could fall, so can I.

Con Artist or Charity Champion?

Greg Mortenson is a celebrity. Even the president of the United States gave $100,000 of his Nobel Prize earnings to Mortenson's charity, the Central Asia Institute (CAI). CAI creates educational opportunities for children in Afghanistan and Pakistan, particularly girls.

More than anyone else, the mountain climber turned champion for the underprivileged brought the plight of central Asia's children to the global stage.

His success was based on a compelling story—one told in his bestselling book, *Three Cups of Tea*. Unfortunately, it turns out his story had a few holes.

First there was the mistaken Taliban reference. Mortenson shares about the time he was held hostage by the Taliban. He has a photo to prove it. The photo of him shows several men identified as his captors.

But it turns out the men in the photo were not the Taliban. *60 Minutes* found that one man, Mansur Khan Mahsud, is a research director of an esteemed Islamabad think tank who has been published in the U.S. He says Mortenson was a guest, not a hostage.

Mahsud says, "This is totally false, and he is lying. He was not kidnapped."[8]

Mortenson admits to some exaggeration in his story.[9] It can be argued that *Three Cups of Tea* and his second book, *Stones Into Schools*, have been great vehicles to spread the word about those in need. But even little steps as simple as embellishing a story for dramatic effect lead to places you never thought you would go.

The media community put Mortenson on trial.

Jon Krakauer, author of *Into Thin Air*, claims that Mortenson was using the organization as a "private ATM machine."[10] Donations were being used for things like personal jets.

Of the thirty schools that *60 Minutes* observed, about half were either no longer being funded or had been abandoned—some were used "to store spinach, or hay for livestock; others had not received any money from Mortenson's charity in years."

Jon Krakauer said, "Mortenson started with noble intentions and a great idea. . . . But very soon after he launched CAI, he lost his moral bearings. He betrayed the trust of countless people, including myself."[11]

Mortenson is not a villain. In fact, he is often described as a quiet, humble man who did work tirelessly on behalf of the poor. Often working twelve- to sixteen-hour days, he would share CAI's message with school groups and at libraries, dinners, and colleges; get on a plane at midnight; and sleep as he flew to the next destination. Once landed, he would hit the ground running and do it all over again.

But in the process of running hard to serve, he made several huge errors of judgment. Today the founder of CAI is no longer the executive director.[12]

Good people doing good things seem to so easily go astray, one small step at a time.

If you believe that "it couldn't happen to me," then you are in the most danger. If you're unaware of temptation, you're vulnerable. In a study of 246 fallen ministry leaders who all confessed to committing sexual immorality

> **If you believe that "it couldn't happen to me," then you are in the most danger.**

within a two-year period, each one said that they had previously believed that it "will never happen to me."[13] They thought they were immune.

I desperately want to figure out how to set up guardrails to protect me from these minor compromises which lead to major blowups.

Small Steps

When Laurel and I were new to Lancaster, we were also new to parenting. And we were discovering what a big job it is to be a parent.

Our first Labor Day in Lancaster, we attended a picnic at the home of our organization's founders, Jeff and Sue Rutt. The Rutts have three children, who ranged from middle school to high school when we first met them. They greeted guests with smiles, served potato salad, and helped little kids learn how to hold a tennis racquet. When it was time for the dishes, they jumped in without needing to be asked.

I was amazed.

Clearly, Jeff and Sue were doing something right. And I wanted to know their secret. What did they do in the kids' early years to help them grow into responsible and helpful young people?

Over lunch a week later, Jeff summarized his parenting philosophy, "When your kids test the limits and step over the line, you have to act. Be consistent. Be loving. But be tough."

Knowing how prone I am to wander away from the One I love makes me want to apply this same recipe in my life and in my home. Be consistent. Be loving. Be tough with even the smallest compromises. If you're firm (and self-aware) when it comes to the minor issues, chances are you'll be much less likely to have to deal with the major ones.

Integrity begins with the small decisions we make each day. By increasing the guards around my heart and continuing to pray that God would protect me from myself, I hope to avoid the pain King David brought on those he loved.

Recognizing the frailty of our own willpower makes me want to earnestly pray with the ancient Psalmist, "Do not let me stray from your commands. I have hidden your word in my heart that I might not sin against you."[14]

And to anyone who heard my gorilla story, I was only dragged ten feet.

Discussion Questions

1. Have you ever exaggerated the truth for a good cause? How?

2. Read 2 Samuel 11. Discuss how David compromised himself to the point of committing adultery and murder.

3. How do you know when you are making small compromises? How do know when your moral compass is broken?

For photos of the gorilla attack, see www.peterkgreer.com/danger/chapter5.

WHAT GOES UP

The Spiritual Danger of Using the Wrong Measuring Stick to Define Success

We need to leave our lusting for ever-larger spheres of Christian service and concentrate on seeing God for ourselves and finding the deep answer for life in Him.

—Roy and Revel Hession

Experts had said it couldn't be done. The country wasn't ready for microfinance. The poor wouldn't repay loans. And the government was too corrupt.

But we saw the Democratic Republic of Congo (Congo) as aligned with our mission to serve in challenging places.

Congo is known for its problems: Ranked the most difficult place in the world to do business for the past five years, it has hosted the most deadly war since World War II,[1] waged in an effort to control vast natural resources. Called "the rape capital

73

of the world," it's a country known for human trafficking and horrific violence against women.[2]

And it's a place that humbled me.

Shortly after joining our organization, I traveled to Kinshasa, where I met the local staff. They had a vision for their country. They saw potential in the hardworking Congolese men and women. And they told me they knew we could make a difference.

We wanted to dream big. At the time, only one in a thousand Congolese had access to a bank. No other faith-based organizations were there to help entrepreneurs start small businesses through access to training and small loans. So we conducted market surveys to understand the needs of our potential clients.

I was there for the program's launch and watched it grow from the ground up—and grow it did.

In August 2004, our team distributed our first loans. Over the next five years, we experienced dizzying growth. Clients were clamoring for our services.

At one point we were adding a thousand clients every month. By December 2008 we were serving almost twenty-four thousand families in a country where everyone told us it could not be done.

I remember thinking, *It's really not that hard. We can actually do this!*

Beyond that, lives were being changed: Entrepreneurs were expanding their businesses. Parents shared how, through increased income, they were able to pay for school fees. And many were returning to the church as they experienced uncommon care and concern from committed staff.

As we grew in the Congo, all our summary indicators pointed to health and vitality.

In just five years, we were a true success story. I presented our accomplishments at microfinance conferences. The World Bank honored our success with a Pro-Poor Innovation Award.

It was as if we could hear God telling us, "Whatever you have in mind, go ahead and do it, for the Lord is with you."[3] We were making a difference. We had built an amazing program from nothing in one of the most challenging places in the world. And we were only a few steps away from discovering fraud, closing branches, laying off staff, and facing a humbling restart of the program.

What Goes Up . . .

After five years of success, we became painfully aware of the fact that we had failed to build a solid foundation.

Driven by a desire to have even greater impact, we (1) expanded beyond our capacity; (2) hadn't developed all the necessary internal controls; and (3) trusted individuals without appropriate checks and balances. We were not built to last. Closing branches and refocusing our efforts, we dismissed over one hundred staff.

It wasn't just about our ministry; it was also about me. I was devastated. I had found a huge piece of my personal and organizational identity in the success of this program.

I had enjoyed being able to say to the naysayers, "Microfinance can succeed anywhere, even in the most difficult corners of the world. Just look at us!"

Going to Washington, D.C., and presenting on our work, I had created a PowerPoint presentation outlining ten steps to implement microfinance in hard places. I previously had all of the answers. Not so much anymore.

What happened? Over the next few years, we explored this question extensively and what we learned has profoundly changed me. Key operational lessons were learned, but the primary danger wasn't the rapid growth, the failure to adequately plan, or even program leadership. It was the state of our hearts.

> *After five years of success, we became painfully aware of the fact that we had failed to build a solid foundation.*

Gateway Sin[4]

Jim Collins, bestselling author of *How the Mighty Fall,* says that the first stage to a company's decline isn't an external factor, but an internal attitude: hubris.

Though a secular writer, Collins recognized that "pride goes before destruction" as the Bible warns in Proverbs.[5] Though pride doesn't necessarily lead to an external blowout, church fathers like Augustine considered pride a precursor to other sins—in essence, pride is a gateway sin.[6]

Turning our hearts away from the Creator, pride causes us to "narcissistically" look to ourselves for what is good, making us believe we are creators, rather than the created, opening ourselves to a variety of other sins: wanting more of the biggest and brightest (greed), objectifying others for sexual pleasure (lust)—chasing good things in an inappropriate way.[7]

With so many other scandals making headlines, pride seems like a minor issue. But pride is the root cause of so much evil.

Ultimately, pride leads us to adopt the wrong definition of success.

Unfortunately, pride is not limited to the sphere of secular business. It's also found in congregations, in soup kitchens— and in ministries that try to help people work their way out of poverty in the Congo.

Ministry of the Big Deal

We had been caught up in a delusion, one that many fall into: As long as our graphs are up and to the right, as long as we have a growing ministry, a bigger congregation, larger amounts of giving, and more good works, we *must* be on the right path.

There's nothing wrong with a bigger ministry or congregation, but a fascination with such markers is toxic.

Author Richard Foster said, "Make no mistake, the religion of the 'big deal' stands in opposition to the way of Christ."[8]

In short: We'd adopted the wrong definition of success.

Just a few days ago, I was at a wedding in Georgia with my friend Kurt. On the way to the wedding was a giant billboard for a church. Front and center of the billboard was the smiling face of the pastor. Underneath his photo was the church's website—which happened to be the pastor's name with .com following it.

Kurt said to me, "I can virtually guarantee that this story will not have a happy ending."

A church with a billboard all about the pastor is a church that is in trouble. The pastor was what was sold and marketed—not Jesus. Our stories will unravel when we are the stars of the story.

The Weeping Prophet

To God, success is upside down. For example, we consider Jeremiah a successful prophet. But for forty years Jeremiah had no results. He had a message no one wanted to hear.

A social outcast and shunned by all, Jeremiah was instructed by God to avoid normal facets of life: weddings, funerals, parties. A bachelor, he couldn't marry or have kids.[9]

Foretelling God's judgment didn't make him very popular. Jeremiah said, "I am ridiculed all day long; everyone mocks me."[10]

Buddies from his hometown—and his own kin—plotted to kill him.[11]

Imprisoned twice, one of the times he languished in a dried-out well, left to starve. Ultimately, he was rescued not by his own people, but by a foreigner. Even the ruthless Nebuchadnezzar, king of Babylon, gave him better treatment than did some of Judah's kings.[12]

Jeremiah died a hostage in a foreign land (Egypt), still preaching truth to people who couldn't stand him.[13]

> **Clearly God has a different measuring stick for success and a different plan to change the world.**

It would be difficult to call this a fruitful ministry.

Jeremiah wasn't the only one who looked like a failure at the end of his life. Still leading an ungrateful and obstinate people, Moses died having never entered the land promised by God. Even Christ didn't look like a success—all Jesus had to show for His years of ministry was eleven cowering disciples.

Clearly God has a different measuring stick for success and a different plan to change the world.

Recovering

Few conversations are more difficult than sharing with your most generous donors that your performance was woefully subpar. Following the restructuring of our program in Congo, that's what happened.

Throughout 2009, we'd been touting Forgotten Africa, a campaign to help expand our services in the most difficult regions of the continent. On paper, we had looked like we had it all together and were poised to leverage our successful record of explosive growth in Congo. That had been our marketing pitch.

And then we had the fallout in Congo in late 2009. It wasn't just the staff with whom we had to share our failings—I knew we needed to share what happened with some of our key supporters as well. I had a pit in my stomach as I boarded the plane and headed to a luncheon with a group of our largest and most influential supporters in Texas.

I felt responsible, and I felt ashamed. I felt I had let everyone down: the hardworking entrepreneurs, the staff, the donors.

But after several hours, this group of supporters was amazingly gracious. They wanted to know how we had responded.

They wanted to hear what we had learned and what we were doing differently as a result. And then they offered words of encouragement about some of their lowest times and how God used even the failures to teach them lifelong lessons.

They echoed something businessman Jim Amos shared: "All we get on the mountaintop is a good view. The real change comes through the hard work of the climb."[14]

After the course correction in Congo, we are rebuilding, slowly and painfully. Our mistakes created opportunities to learn and provided a perspective I hope I never forget—we need a strong foundation and a fanatical obsession with operational excellence, but most of all we need to continually have a spirit of humble dependence upon God.

We need a new definition of success.

Ambition God's Way

When we measure our success based solely on outputs and comparison to others, we are undoubtedly heading in the wrong direction. It's easy to equate the Lord's "blessing" with how many (or how few) people follow me on Twitter, know me by name, and want me to speak at their event. Doing so, I adopt a skewed definition of success.

We do the same thing when we become enamored with churches with the highest growth rates and forget to examine the depth of character of the leaders. It's possible to build a mega-ministry and feel so good about "our success" that we also develop a mega-ego. It's almost impossible to overstate the importance of humility. As pastor Jon Tyson put it, "When our influence exceeds our character, we are heading toward a disaster."[15]

I see a very different example in the life of Jesus. Christ's life and ministry stood in stark contrast to spiritual self-promotion and obsession with numbers. Instead of clamoring for success, the Redeemer came to earth to serve and took the nature of a servant, not a superstar.

Jesus defined success as loving the Lord your God and loving your neighbor. The extent of our love, not numerical growth, matters most. One of Jesus' biggest criticisms of the religious is that they adopted the wrong definition of success. They believed they were successful if they were given "the most important seats in the synagogues" and were recognized as esteemed teachers.[16]

> *Instead of clamoring for success, the Redeemer came to earth to serve and took the nature of a servant, not a superstar.*

No longer was their desire for Scripture about wanting to be close to God; it had translated into desiring notoriety for themselves. Success had become an obsession, an idol, their object of worship.

Contrast this to those changed by Christ in the New Testament. You see that they weren't obsessed with searching for significance—with fame or fortune—but they were obsessed with embracing their identity in Christ.

They called attention to their heritage—they were the sons and daughters of the King. They didn't seem to call much attention to themselves and continually diverted attention to their Savior.

Instead of comparing ourselves to others, let's recognize our identity in Christ. Then we can determine whether we're being faithful with what we have been given, and let go of our spiritually dangerous preoccupation with worldly success.

Discussion Questions

1. What ways has your background influenced the way you personally think about success? How has this been good and/or harmful?

2. What is dangerous about adopting the wrong definition of success?

3. Read Micah 6:6–8. How does God define success for an individual's life according to the passage?

To see a video of the lessons learned from adopting the wrong definition of success in Congo, see www.peterkgreer.com/danger /chapter6.

7

3 A.M. FRIENDS

The Spiritual Danger of Friendship Superficiality

Faithful are the wounds of a friend,
But deceitful are the kisses of an enemy.

—Proverbs 27:6 NASB

My friend Dave[1] is an up-and-coming pastor in Virginia. In the past few years he has experienced remarkable growth in his church. Today, it serves thousands. It is engaged in missions and actively serves the local community.

Dave is happily married, but a few years ago a younger woman at his church began to give him a lot of attention. Not only was she attractive, but Dave realized he was enjoying her attention and friendship.

Having the self-awareness to recognize that this was a potentially unhealthy situation, Dave went to the elders of his church. He told them about this woman. He described the way their friendship was growing. But he went beyond confession. He gave an invitation.

He asked them to hold him accountable.

Humbly he told them, "I need your help with this." They listened. And they said they would help.

Time went by. But the elders never reached out.

So he brought it before them again. He again extended an invitation. And again they consented.

But to this day, not one of them has ever asked him about the relationship.

True Accountability Partners

"Accountability" is a buzz word in the church but it's easier to talk about than it is to implement, particularly for those who are seen as doing good.

Today, we are still shocked when prominent pastors and ministry leaders make major mistakes, but it's really not that shocking if we believe we all struggle with sin until the day Jesus returns. We are all just one decision away from a major mess.

It's spiritually unhealthy to put people who do good up on a shaky pedestal and believe that they must have greater immunity to temptation. It's also not being a good friend.

Five summers ago, one of my good friends, Brian,[2] invited Laurel and me to go to California with him to enjoy beaches, vineyards, and views of the Pacific from an isolated home on the coast. It would be the vacation of a lifetime. And we would be traveling with him and his girlfriend.

Last minute, Laurel and I needed to cancel. But Brian did not want to miss this amazing opportunity. So he and his girlfriend went alone.

Right before the trip, I had a chance to talk to Brian. My gut instinct told me to tell him that what he was doing wasn't wise.

This was a honeymoon trip—except that the wedding hadn't taken place yet. But I didn't ask him about the trip. Brian is one of the godliest and most faith-filled men I know, and I didn't want to have a potentially awkward conversation. Even though he had invited me to be one of his "accountability partners," he probably didn't really need me to be involved in his personal life, right?

They took the trip. A year later, Brian and his girlfriend were engaged. And things were going well. But before the wedding, they called it off.

On the day of his wedding, instead of getting married, Brian was sitting around a campfire with me and another friend trying to diagnose what went wrong. He spoke of the hurt of this loss and mentioned that the trip to California was not the wisest decision.

Sitting at the campfire, we realized we had failed our friend. He had asked us to provide accountability, but just like Dave's elders, we hadn't come through. He invited us to be real friends and ask some tough questions, but we didn't.

Walking on Water at 3 A.M.

In literature, art, and pop culture, 3 a.m. is when you hit rock bottom.

The song that launched the career for the King of Blues, B. B. King, was "3 O'Clock Blues." It was a suicidal lament. Eminem and many other artists have followed suit and written about this dark hour.

> *Jesus decided to intervene at 3 a.m., the moment of their greatest need.*

In Scripture we also see an interesting episode at 3 a.m. The disciples were out at sea, and at "about three o'clock in the morning Jesus came toward them, walking on the water."[3]

Why did Jesus go to them? Focusing on Jesus' miracle, we often forget why He was walking on water in the first place.

In the middle of the lake, the disciples were stranded. They couldn't get to shore. By 3 a.m., they were struggling, exhausted with the fight . . . about ready to give up.[4]

At the lowest point of their night, Jesus walked right into the middle of the lake. He calmed the storm. He took them back to shore.

Jesus decided to intervene at 3 a.m., the moment of their greatest need.

Call for 3 A.M. Friends

At twenty-four, as I was just starting to work in relief and development, I landed in Vietnam on a layover. My next flight was canceled, which gave me another day in an unexplored city.

My good friends know that I'm never one to miss anything free. If there are free pretzels offered on the plane, even if I'm not hungry, I'm taking them and storing them for later.

So when the hotel offered a "free massage," I was definitely saying yes.

In the early afternoon, I took the elevator down to the basement of the hotel. I entered a long corridor of small, hospital-white rooms, each with nothing but a single table in the center.

Handed a blue smock and blue booties, I went into a room, put them on, and waited for my masseuse.

When my masseuse entered, she greeted me in broken English. Pouring the oil, she began the massage. Everything was going well. I was starting to relax and forget about my upcoming work schedule.

But near the end of our half-hour session, she changed her tactics. Calling me a "beautiful man," she gave me her number and told me she would finish the massage in my room.

Umm . . . this sort of a situation wasn't in my new employee manual for our Christian relief and development organization.

I went back to my room (alone) and vowed never again to have a massage in another country. But more than that, I longed for 3 a.m. friends who would live life with me and would know if I was making decisions that would lead me away from a devoted life of service to Christ. Friends who would drop everything if I called them in the middle of the night needing their counsel. Friends who'd be praying for me weekly and regularly asking how I was *really* doing. Friends with authority and the invitation to speak truth into my life.

Intervention at 3 A.M.

Jesus saw when the disciples were at their weakest, at their most vulnerable, and stepped in. Christ modeled what friendship should look like.

Whether I'm in Vietnam on a layover or working late at night on my computer, I know myself well enough to see my need for friends who are willing to walk into the middle of the lake. These are the friends on speed dial. Thoroughly unimpressed with anything I've ever done—and knowing the reality of my sin—they love me and accept me anyway. Loving me enough to call me out on my heart's self-deceptions, they don't let me get away with justification and excuses.

I desperately need 3 a.m. friends.

A well-known pastor described how when he travels, one of his friends has permission to call at 11 p.m. just to check in and make sure he isn't doing anything stupid. That's a 3 a.m. friend.

While friendship should flow naturally, this pastor had to be intentional about inviting his friends to be part of his life in this way. These kinds of friends are critical to living well now.

Carrying out a study of fallen ministry leaders, Dr. Howard Hendricks of Dallas Theological Seminary interviewed 246 individuals who'd had a moral failing within a two-year period. He sought to determine key factors that led to their fall.

What he found was striking: None of them had an accountability partner.[5]

If you have trouble identifying your 3 a.m. friends, then chances are you probably don't have them. Now is a great time to invite others to really know you.

Circle of Trust

If you look in Scripture, you see that Jesus had several groups of friends. Jesus had His three closest friends (James, John, and Peter), He had His twelve disciples, and He had a group of seventy people whom He often traveled with. I wanted to use Christ's example in how I invested in my friends. I literally have drawn up three concentric circles with names of people in each of them.

In the center of my diagram are my 3 a.m. friends, whom I can truly call at any time and for any reason. The best part of these friends is that they don't wait for me to call—they actively reach out regularly. If I haven't had a conversation in the past week with any of my 3 a.m. friends, it's time for me to pick up the phone.

The next circle is my band of brothers. David had his mighty men and I have mine. These are people who have my back. Extending from college friends to small-group friendships, this broader group has known me for years. We are unafraid to challenge each other—and provide words of encouragement or rebuke when they're needed. On a monthly basis, I'm regularly interacting with these friends.

And the third circle is my broader community of friends.

They are our neighbors, colleagues, and church friends. Through their friendships, life is fuller, more complete. While they have different functions, all three groups are crucial to being healthy relationally.

In clearly identifying these levels of friendships, I'm intentional about having people who really know me. Otherwise, it's easy to have myriad acquaintances, but no one who truly knows me or my struggles. We need to go way beyond "Facebook friend" status and enter into real relationships where we are deeply known.

Whether or not you actually draw out a diagram, I'd encourage you to identify your 3 a.m. friends.

Warning: Accountability takes time. Many of us don't have a lot of time, so we don't find true accountability. But make the effort. More than anything else deep friendships influence the building of our character. A lack of accountability—as a result of shallow relationships—can wreck us.

As the writer of Proverbs advises, "Whoever walks with the wise becomes wise, but the companion of fools will suffer harm."[6]

Sitting at the campfire on the day he was supposed to be married, Brian reminded us of his need for us to be his 3 a.m. friends. He recognized he couldn't walk the walk alone. And he wasn't meant to.

> *More than anything else deep friendships influence the building of our character.*

Today Brian and I don't just talk about accountability, but we are transparent with each other. In our conversations, everything is on the table. From relationship challenges to our deepest frustrations or feelings of inadequacy, to issues too sensitive to discuss with anyone else, nothing is off limits.

The point is that there is no immunity to temptation for people who do good—we all need 3 a.m. friends to love us at our lowest and protect us from ourselves.

Discussion Questions

1. A 3 a.m. friend as discussed in the chapter is a friend that you can call at any time, one that will truly hold you accountable. Have you ever experienced a time when you needed to call on a 3 a.m. friend?

2. Accountability is often a buzz word in the church. Have you found accountability as an important part of the church that you're in? Why or why not?

3. Jesus had several circles of friends, with just three friends in His inner circle. Can you identify those 3 a.m. friends in your own life?

4. How do you invite people in your life to become part of your core group of friends?

5. What are ways that will help you to be accountable to others in your church community?

For the diagram of the Circle of Trust, see www.peterkgreer .com/danger/chapter7.

8

GOD LOVES MY JOB MORE THAN YOURS

The Spiritual Danger of Elevating the Sacred Over the Secular

It is the business of the Church to recognize that the secular vocation, as such, is sacred.

—Dorothy Sayers

Over a bowl of steaming cabbage borsht in Moscow, I had a conversation that changed the course of my life.

Every international business major at Messiah College (my alma mater) is required to participate in the International Business Institute. This ten-week summer experience exposes students to multinational corporations, central banks, and intense study throughout Europe and Russia with students from a dozen other colleges and universities.

In the second week of the trip, we arrived in Red Square when Boris Yeltsin was campaigning for president. We had choice seats for a key moment in history.

While in Moscow, we also had a casual lunch with a diverse group of missionaries serving in Russia. Seated next to me was a man helping to energize the business community after the Iron Curtain fell. He described his interests in business and ministry and how this tool called microfinance brought these two interests together.

I was hooked. It just made sense that helping a woman set up a fishing business was better than merely handing out fish to those in need.

From that moment, all my papers and research projects centered on this method of economic development that helped families work their way out of poverty and equipped local churches to serve their own communities. My academic advisor, Dr. Ron Webb, fueled my interest and graciously dreamed with me about what a career in this sector would look like.

When I graduated, I was filled with enthusiasm. I wrote passionate cover letters and sent them to every organization I knew that was doing faith-based microfinance. I was willing to go anywhere. Do anything. And I didn't need a salary; I just craved an experience.

Then I waited. And waited. And waited.

Finally, I received a response. It was a postcard saying, "Thank you for applying. We will keep your resume on file for future openings that might be of interest to you." No other organizations even wrote back.

Not a good sign.

I reluctantly moved in with my parents back in Massachusetts when I was ready to move overseas. Moving back in with your parents: the dream of every ambitious college graduate. It was painfully obvious that it was time to start working on Plan B.

Plan B took shape over another meal. At a prayer breakfast, I met the headmaster of a private academy in Lexington, Massachusetts, Dr. Barry Koops. Instead of borsht in Moscow, I ate fruit and yogurt in downtown Boston. Instead of learning about microfinance, I learned about his opening for an assistant business manager who would work with accounts payable/receivable, budgeting, payroll, and financial aid. They needed the position filled immediately.

I interviewed within a week and started right away. Although I was thankful to have a job, in the back of my mind, I felt like I was compromising. A fantastic role at a great school, but—in my line of thinking—it was a second-tier option. My heart was in international missions. And besides, serving the poor overseas was a higher calling than serving high school students in Lexington, Massachusetts, right?

I had bought into a false and hazardous hierarchy of service. In my hierarchy, overseas ministry was at the top of the pyramid. Next was full-time Christian service in the U.S. Then came the honorable professions, like being a doctor, teacher, or social worker.

An elevated view of full-time ministry is thoroughly unbiblical.

My perspective was reinforced by my family lineage. My maternal grandfather was a pastor in Philadelphia in a historic stone church in Roxborough. My paternal grandfather was an opera singer who came to Christ and then toured churches singing and reciting Scripture (he memorized almost the entire New Testament). With my dad also a pastor, I have full-time ministry in my DNA.

But an elevated view of full-time ministry is thoroughly unbiblical. Sabotaging our ability to impact the world for Christ, it leaves most of the church on the sidelines, cheering on the pastors and missionaries.

Insiders vs. Outsiders

When God decided to announce His arrival to the world, the Savior skipped the religious and went straight for the blue-collar workers, the shepherds.

In *Kingdom Calling*, author Amy Sherman unpacks Proverbs 11:10 and details how "When the righteous prosper, the city rejoices." The majority of the righteous—those who know God's heart—are not working in the temple. Rather they work within the city in every sort of occupation. When they flourish in honoring God through their work, there is major celebration.

The whole community benefits when we see our ministry as being integrated into everyday life, not just Sunday morning.

Consider the CEO who helps to employ a thousand people in a town suffering from economic depression.

Or the doctor who serves Medicaid patients, even if it's not as lucrative to take care of the poor.

Or the elementary schoolteacher who helps students to read in an area where illiteracy is high.

These are stories that need to be celebrated. Despite the biblical examples where God is at work in all professions, I regularly see interns with their heads down and their hearts saddened when they take a "normal job" in the private sector. They feel like they're compromising if they are unable to do full-time Christian service. Or I hear executives who want to transition from success to significance by becoming a leader at a ministry. And they feel disappointed when the doors do not open right away. They feel they are settling by staying in the private sector for a few more years.

These feelings are fueled by the spiritual danger of elevating full-time service. When we think full-time ministry is some sort of a higher calling, we dramatically undermine our calling and impact as followers of Jesus.

In a forty-year span, we devote 96,000 hours to our jobs, and only 2,266 hours at church, noted Adam Hamilton, a pastor from Church of the Resurrection (COR) in Leawood, Kansas.[1]

Speaking directly to his megachurch, Hamilton said, "If 12,000 of us realize that we're missionaries first and we go out into our workaday world everyday on a mission to bless, to love, to heal, to bring justice, to serve God in the workplace—then when we finally begin to do that, I tell you, the world is going to be different."[2]

If there is such a thing as full-time ministry, we're all in it. God's mission agency includes bankers, nurses, and bricklayers.

Tear Down This Wall

I want to reclaim Abraham Kuyper's bold stance of smashing the divide between the sacred and the secular.

Kuyper was a PK (pastor's kid) who lived during the nineteenth century and early twentieth century. Although he followed in his father's footsteps as pastor of a Dutch Reformed Church for the town of Beesd, he felt called to impact the world through politics.

Leaving "full-time ministry," he took to the political sphere, eventually becoming prime minister of the Netherlands. He also spent time as a journalist and a theologian. Through his work as a journalist, he helped to revive the Christian community. Through his work as a political leader, he helped to reform education.

> *Jesus is calling you to use your gifts to share the Good News in whichever aspect of society you are most gifted to serve.*

His faith was central, whether he was a pastor or a politician.

His most famous quote, "In the total expanse of human life there is not a single square inch of which the Christ, who alone is sovereign, does not declare, 'That is mine!'"[3]

You don't have to be a full-time pastor to live and share the Gospel. Not everyone was made to be a pastor, to teach, or to lead worship. Paul summarizes, "For just as each of us has one body with many members, and these members do not all have the same function, so in Christ we, though many, form one body, and each member belongs to all the others."[4]

Jesus is calling you to use your gifts to share the Good News in whichever aspect of society you are most gifted to serve.

Crocheting and Changing Lives

One way the lines between ministry and business are being blurred is through the rise of social entrepreneurship. I recently had the opportunity to spend time with Kohl Crecelius, a social entrepreneur in his mid-twenties, at Praxis, a gathering of young social entrepreneurs.

In high school, Kohl liked crocheting. So he taught his two best friends. Dubbed the Krochet Kids, together they knitted and sold enough beanies to make money for an epic prom night—complete with a hot-air balloon ride with their prom dates.

When they went off to different colleges, they forgot about crocheting. Then Kohl's friend Stewart went to Uganda. Coming back, he recounted how people were living in desperate conditions in camps and had one consistent request, "Please help us find a job."

"This idea of crocheting came up, but I was pretty skeptical," Kohl said. "I didn't think it was something the world needed. I wanted something bigger, something more broad."[5]

But they tried it out. Soon the three of them were teaching ten women in Uganda government camps how to knit. Now one hundred ladies are making hats in Uganda. Operating in both Peru and Uganda, Krochet Kids sells hats and clothes—each signed by the woman who made it—at Nordstrom and other high-end retailers, as well as online.

Something as simple as crocheting is changing lives.

Master Craftsman

When we think of the Tabernacle in the Old Testament, we often think of priests, incense, and sacrifices. We don't think of artisans and skilled laborers having a part.

But when God called for the building of the Tabernacle, it wasn't only the priests the Creator called. He also specifically empowered artists and craftsmen.

God chose Bezalel to build the sanctuary. So God "filled him with the Spirit of God, with wisdom, with understanding, with knowledge and with all kinds of skills—to make artistic designs for work in gold, silver and bronze."[6]

He gave Bezalel a high calling. Breathing His Spirit into Bezalel, God gifted him just as He empowered Moses to be a leader and Miriam to be a prophetess.

We reflect a Master Craftsman. It makes sense that God would also use our creative talents and abilities, just like He uses gifts of preaching and leading worship. It is time to encourage the full range of creative gifts and skills within our church body.

People who do not buy into the sacred/secular divide are the ones impacting all society. A great example is my friends Alan and Katherine.

Kingdom Business

Every Saturday morning, Alan and Katherine Barnhart eat pancakes with their children. I had the privilege of joining them for their weekly ritual. Alan makes the pancakes—and they are golden brown and served with peanut butter and real maple syrup (try it!). But you have to work for them. Flinging pancakes across the room, Alan makes you catch them on your plate before you eat.

From their modest, family-oriented lifestyle, you'd never guess they own a huge company that combines engineering genius with MacGyver innovation to move buildings, power plants, wind turbines, and other items few companies in the world could transport.

Alan has a calling in business. Focused and persistent, Alan pursues excellence in everything he does. When I visited his headquarters, it was obvious he knew his employees and deeply cared about them as individuals. When he walks into a room, his employees come over to talk and it's clear his team respects him. When they talk, Alan looks them in the eye. He listens. For Alan, this isn't just a job; it's a vocation.

The Barnharts are the first ones to admit they're not perfect. But providing employment for over nine hundred people, they are having an impact as they model what a Christ-centered life looks like.

Additionally, a long time ago Alan and Katherine set a financial finish line—capping their income at a middle-class salary. If God decided to bless them financially, they would give the rest away. They put their company into a charitable trust. They do not own it but they are stewards of the company.

Today over 50 percent of their profits go directly to a fund that is invested in the work of Christian mission organizations. The investment decisions are made by a team at the company, and over fifty people, including some spouses, are involved in the process.

But this almost didn't happen. When Alan, a committed Christian, graduated from college, friends advised him to do "something significant"—to go into full-time ministry.

After working a few years in business with his dad, Alan and Katherine, his fiancée at the time, decided to become missionaries in Saudi Arabia.

God had other plans. As they prepared to leave, Alan's father gave him a proposition: Since he was retiring, he offered the business to Alan and his brother. If Alan wanted to go to Saudi Arabia, his father would sell it to someone else.

Alan and Katherine prayed. More than twenty-five years later, they are still faithfully serving from Tennessee. Through business, God has blessed them.

But His blessing has been far more than financial. When Alan and Katherine decided to cap their income, they invited their company to be part of Kingdom work.

The first year, the Barnhart family and their colleagues gave $50,000. Praying together, they felt called to give it internationally. The next year, they gave $150,000. By the early 2000s, they were giving away $1 million a year.

In 2003, a salesman set an audacious goal: What if the company gave away $1 million a month? By 2005 they had met the goal, and they try to exceed it every year.

"Giving has been great fun," says Alan. "I'm convinced it is much more fun to be a giver than a consumer."

I have learned a lot from the Barnhart family about how to invest in people. How to make family a priority. How delicious pancakes taste when topped with peanut butter and syrup. But I've also seen what happens when we smash the hierarchy of service and ministry.

> *There's an awakening in the church to realize that our day jobs are ministry.*

Whether through social entrepreneurship or through those like the Barnharts who feel called to business—there's an awakening in the church to realize that our day jobs are ministry.

No longer is the best method of evangelism through revivals at arenas and football stadiums, says Dr. Billy Graham. "I believe one of the next great moves of God is going to be through the believers in the workplace," said Graham.[7]

If you are a follower of Jesus, you are already in full-time ministry, no matter where you spend your days.

Discussion Questions

1. Have you ever experienced the false hierarchy of Christian service? If so, why do you think many elevate the sacred calling over the secular?

2. How has God uniquely gifted you?

3. Read Exodus 35:30–36:2. How did God empower craftspeople to bring Him glory?

4. When have you used your gifts to bring glory to God?

To watch a video of Alan sharing his story, see www.peterkgreer .com/danger/chapter8.

9

WORM FOOD

The Spiritual Danger of Thinking You're the Superhero in Your Story

I am constantly surprised at how I keep taking the gifts God has given me—my health, my intellectual and emotional gifts—and keep using them to impress people, receive affirmation and praise, and compete for rewards, instead of developing them for the glory of God.[1]

—Henri Nouwen

Acknowledgments

When I open a book, I flip to the end and read the acknowledgments first. Yes, it's weird. But after writing *The Poor Will Be Glad*, I recognize that no one writes a book alone. It may take a village to raise a child, but it takes a SWAT team of editors, writers, friends, and colleagues to write a book.

Although it would be socially acceptable to say *The Spiritual Danger of Doing Good* is by Peter Greer—that these are my stories—that would only be part of the truth.

Three years ago an intern named Anna came to our ministry after graduating from Asbury University. She majored in English and has skills in writing that I don't. During her internship, she listened to my voicemails from the road and crafted them into coherent stories. I sent her notes, and she would turn them into blog posts or presentations. When her internship ended, we hired her, and she now provides major help with everything I write. She probably edited this sentence.

But it is not only Anna who made this book possible. We would not have finished this book on time if we hadn't discovered our incredible intern Allie. Allie is a remarkable woman who, despite battling cancer, researched and wrote furiously for months (even from the hospital while getting treatment).

But Anna, Allie, and I would not have a book if it were not for our amazing agent, Andrew Wolgemuth, or Andy McGuire and the team at Bethany House. I tried self-publishing with a children's book titled *Mommy's Heart Went POP!* and I now realize how critical a team of professionals is to creating a book. And the list goes on and on (please do read the acknowledgments to know all the people who made this book possible).

This same issue of reliance on others spills over into every area of life. I'm convinced there are no solo performances.

At HOPE International, anything good we have accomplished can be traced to Jesse Casler. I offered Jesse a job even before I officially started, and he quickly became a true friend and invaluable advisor. A former banker from Boston, Jesse is the type of guy who likes to read prospectuses on the weekends. He makes my habit of reading acknowledgments first seem normal!

Without Jesse's attention to detail, our ministry would be in disarray.

In moments of clarity, it is easy to see how dependent we are on others, but why is it so easy to take credit for someone else's hard work? Why do we crave to be the superhero in our story, especially when we're doing good? And how might God feel when we take credit for what He has done?

Look at What I Did!

My kids love fishing. On a typical Sunday afternoon, we're at a local lake with bobbers, worms, and tangled lines.

On one fishing trip my son Keith took a break from fishing and decided to try to catch tadpoles with his net. I picked up his rod, threw out the line, and after a few moments the bobber disappeared. I set the line and started reeling it to shore.

"Keith, come here!" I shouted. He dropped his net and came running.

Reeling in the last few feet, Keith raised a small sunfish. Not a huge catch, but he was ecstatic.

Keith proudly held up the fish, saying to his brother and sister, "Look at the fish I caught!"

> *How might God feel when we take credit for what he has done?*

Despite the fact that he hadn't cast, hadn't waited, hadn't set the hook, and just arrived for the final few moments, he believed that he'd caught the fish.

It's cute when our kids do this. It's offensive when we do it with God.

Hey, God, look at the way I tithe!
Hey, God, look at how I serve at soup kitchens every week!
Hey, God, look at the people singing songs I wrote!
Hey, God, listen to the sermon I preached!
Hey, God, look at me!

I wonder if God, as a loving father, laughs and says, "You just showed up to reel in the final few feet."

In one of Aesop's fables, a similar idea is conveyed. A flea sitting on the back of a chariot looks back and says, "My, what a dust storm I've caused."[2]

It's easy to give ourselves credit that is truly due to God. We seem to be hardwired to take credit and be in the spotlight of our good deeds.

In the Middle Ages, Thomas Aquinas recognized the propensity of do-gooders for vainglory—one of the seven deadly sins. An obsessed and "disordered" love of praise, vainglory is an offshoot of pride. People pleasers at heart, people who are doing good are predisposed to develop praise addictions. Service-oriented types often feel entitled to receive honor for the good they do.[3]

But really what's the harm in a little recognition?

Fatal Mistake

Most likely Acts 12 is not the kind of story you grew up learning in Sunday school and coloring pictures of for your fridge. I can guarantee few parents use it as a bedtime story.

This is because if they did, it would sound something like this:

> Once upon a time, there was a king. His name was Herod. King Herod had an announcement for the people in his kingdom. After completing his announcement, his people thought he did such a good job that they began to clap their hands and praise King Herod.
>
> They said that he spoke so well that he must be a god. Accepting their praise, Herod neglected to tell them God was the one deserving glory. This upset God. According to Scripture, "Immediately, because Herod did not give praise to God, an angel of the Lord struck him down, and he was eaten by worms and died."[4]

Not exactly the kind of story that will send you off to a good night's sleep. This is a scene out of a horror movie. A man is eaten alive by worms, and it is all because he simply did nothing.

Herod didn't tell the people to praise him and give him all the credit; he simply didn't correct them when they did. This may seem like a trivial mistake, but it's not.

Herod stood in God's rightful place of glory. Herod had a sovereignty problem.

Naked for Jesus

Just a few pages after the story of King Herod, in Acts 14, we find a very similar story with a very different ending. Paul and Barnabas encountered a man in Lystra who was lame. Paul told him to get up and walk. And he did. Incredulous, the crowd sought to worship them. Hailing them as the Greek gods Zeus and Hermes, the crowd brought animals and wreaths to offer Paul and Barnabas sacrifices.

What was Paul and Barnabas's reaction?

They ripped their clothes and shouted to emphatically direct the attention back to God. They attributed the miracles to Him. He was the one who had healed, not they.[5]

Paul and Barnabas faced a situation similar to Herod's. These contrasting stories showcase two polar opposite approaches to praise: (1) Take the credit for the work of God; or (2) Rip our clothes and shout until people understand that anything good we have or do is from God.

Get Over Yourself

"When I first arrived in Kenya, I wanted a pat on the back just for leaving my cushy job in the U.S. and showing up," my friend

Courtney Rountree Mills says to young, eager-to-save-the-world staff and volunteers.

"But, what you will soon learn is that it is not our job to 'save' anyone. Only Jesus can save."

Courtney co-founded a nonprofit, Sinapis, to provide Christ-centered business training and investment capital to innovative, highly scalable start-ups in Kenya.

"If you first get over yourself, stop expecting praise for everything that you do, and decide to serve for no other reason than to serve God alone, it will change your life," Courtney says.

> *In our culture so focused on praise, it's important to recognize that we need to get over ourselves if we want to make a difference.*

In our culture so focused on praise, it's important to recognize that we need to get over ourselves if we want to make a difference.

Are we hopeless addicts to praise with superhero complexes?

Center Stage

The fastest way to break the superhero complex is what author Richard Foster calls the "ministry of the small things."[6] Forget the center stage. Don't clamor for the spotlight. Far from the press, uncover God in small, unseen, and unrewarded acts of compassion.

Author François Fénelon says,

> When the occasion for you to do something great comes, it has its own rewards: the excitement, the respect gained from others, and the pride that will accompany your ability to do such "great" things.
>
> To do small things that are right continually, without being noticed, is much more important. These small acts attack your pride, your laziness, your self-centeredness, and your oversensitive nature. It is much more appealing to make great sacrifices to God,

however hard they might be, so that you might do whatever you want with the small decisions of life. Faithfulness in the little things better proves your true love for God. It is the slow, plodding path rather than a passing fit of enthusiasm that matters.[7]

While doing great things has its own rewards, the ministry of small things leads to faithful living. We don't need to tweet about them or post them on Facebook, but small acts of obedience to the Father are big acts in the Kingdom.

Laurel's grandmother Muffy was a champion of the little things. Writing hundreds of letters throughout her lifetime, Muffy offered encouragement and hope to those in need. Muffy's cards—with artwork handcrafted on fine stationery—were not only thoughtful, but also an expression of love.

When the mother of our friend Ginny died over ten years ago, Muffy wrote a letter to Ginny. Muffy didn't know her very well but understood grief. Early in her marriage, just after giving birth to their second daughter, Muffy lost her husband. Understanding loss, Muffy was able to encourage Ginny.

Just a few weeks after Muffy died, Laurel and I discovered this letter. Ginny, who had treasured the letter in her time of mourning, sent it to Laurel. When Laurel read Muffy's words of comfort, it was as if Muffy were speaking just to her, sustaining her through her loss. More than any other words or actions, this letter helped Laurel to mourn and to celebrate the gift of her precious grandmother.

It is the little things done with no pomp or fanfare that seem to matter most.

Love Sick

"If you don't know you are the beloved, you will have to be the star of every story," said Pastor Jon Tyson of Trinity Grace Church in New York City.[8]

Why do we seek praise? Ultimately, we are afraid deep down we're not good enough. So we use cheap glitter to hide our true selves.

Unless we know we are loved, unless we turn our eyes away from ourselves to our Creator and recognize that we are complete and whole through Christ, we feel the need to continue striving for acceptance.

Musicians who make it big are not often known for their humility, but Ryan O'Neal is an exception. His band Sleeping at Last is experiencing a flurry of success and accolades. A gifted songwriter and performer, Ryan's music has been featured on movies like the blockbuster hit *Twilight: Breaking Dawn—Part 1* and shows like *So You Think You Can Dance.* But what I admire most about Ryan is not his success or his abilities, but the way in which he receives praise. After a concert, I watched him interact with raving fans who wanted to tell him how great he was and how his music influenced their lives.

> When we turn our eyes away from ourselves, we see that we're not the superheroes—but we're part of a much bigger story than we ever could have dreamed.

Ryan genuinely expressed gratitude for each comment and did so without even a hint of arrogance. It was obvious his life didn't depend on the affection of others, and he neither gloated in the spotlight nor let praise from others inflate his ego. He typically just genuinely responded, "That is really kind—thank you very much." Free to simply be grateful for the kindness of his fans, he didn't cling to the praise and affection of others. He knew he was a small part of a bigger story.

Breaking free of our inflated view of ourselves comes when we ruminate on the amazing story told in Scripture. When we orient our view toward God's glory, we get a glimpse of the grand story, one of redemption of wholeness and hope from a very big God. As another songwriter wrote many years ago:

When I consider your heavens,
    the work of your fingers,
the moon and the stars,
    which you have set in place,
what is mankind that you are mindful of them,
    human beings that you care for them?[9]

When we turn our eyes away from ourselves, we see that we're not the superheroes—but we're part of a much bigger story than we ever could have dreamed.

You and I make lousy superheroes and lousier saviors. And we probably don't look too good in full-body spandex either.

The Virtuoso

Recognized as one of the greatest composers of all time, Johann Sebastian Bach was also a devout Christ-follower. His life's maxim: All gifts are from God and for God.

And he wanted to make sure that each piece of music helped him remember this fact.

At the beginning of each piece, Bach would write *Jesu Juva*[10]— Jesus help me. Closing every manuscript, he signed S.D.G., shorthand for *Soli Deo Gloria*—glory to God alone.[11]

In this simple visual reminder, he declared that it was not his talent, nor his innovation and work ethic that deserved praise. Bach understood that he was solely dependent on God's Spirit for everything (*Jesu Juva*). And everything he created gave God fame (*Soli Deo Gloria*).

Jesus, help us remember that anything good that happens is for your glory.

Discussion Questions

    1. How does the desire for fame play out in our spiritual lives?

2. Was there ever a time that someone took credit for something that you did? How did that make you feel?

3. What are some tangible ways that we can give credit to God as we go, give, and serve?

4. Often it's the "ministry of the small things" that helps us to break a habit of desiring praise. What is one way someone has ministered to you or a friend in a small yet meaningful gesture?

5. Think of several ways you can carry out an act of kindness or generosity this week without the receiver knowing about it.

For a video of Ryan O'Neal from Sleeping at Last, see www .peterkgreer.com/danger/chapter9.

10

PANERA PROPHET

The Spiritual Danger of Not Having Ears to Hear the Uncomfortable Truth

But he said to me, "My grace is sufficient for you, for my power is made perfect in weakness." Therefore I will boast all the more gladly about my weaknesses, so that Christ's power may rest on me. . . . For when I am weak, then I am strong.[1]

—Paul

Less than a mile from our office is Panera Bread. With its inviting ambiance, Panera is a natural place for regular meetings.

Panera gets atmosphere. Walking in the front door, you are immediately hit by the smells of freshly baked bread. Tan and burgundy colors and muted lighting are designed to make you feel as warm as the coffee mug in your hands. It's a place you expect to have conversations and coffee. *It's not a place you expect to meet a prophet.*

111

As I walked into Panera, I sat down with a friend ready for casual conversation. But on this particular day, we skipped the small talk.

Greg looked straight at me and asked how I was doing. And I told him. I described to him how my family life wasn't quite like it used to be, how I wasn't feeling appreciated, and some ways I was struggling.

He listened intently. He asked questions. But then he did something unusual. He called me on my attitudes and actions.

Good friends sympathize. Good friends relate. But good friends also challenge. And on this particular day, he knew that I didn't need sympathy; I needed a kick in the butt.

Greg is the type of friend the author of Proverbs describes, "Wounds from a friend can be trusted, but an enemy multiplies kisses."[2] Greg was a good enough friend to inflict a few healing wounds. He said what I needed to hear. People who do good can be inappropriately held up as an example and desperately need people in our lives who are totally unimpressed with our service. I needed Greg to call me on my unhealthy thoughts and actions.

Without exaggeration or drama, he described how my attitude and behaviors would affect my family and my faith. He outlined where my ruts were heading.

Greg looks normal, but he was following the footsteps of biblical leaders wrapped in capes and walking with staffs who provided prophetic critique. They burned plows, ripped their clothes, cooked food over dung, and called down fire from heaven to get their points across. They fiercely proclaimed the Word of God—and it often meant direct criticism when the people of God left their first love.

While we don't have prophets today in quite the same way, we have a desperate need for prophetic critique in our lives, *especially* when we are doing good. This is more than just having people we trust enough to invite into our mess. It is paying attention when people love us enough to challenge us.

I needed a prophetic critique, and it just happened to occur at Panera.

Encounter With a Prophet

You have two choices when you are called out by a prophet, critic, or friend: to ignore the call or to recognize the seriousness of your rut. To make excuses and minimize the issue or to realize a loving critique is a gift and an invitation to change.

In the epic history of Israel, we see this played out when a prophet is sent to Israel's first two kings.

While externally King David and King Saul appeared like they had a lot in common, how they responded to the prophet's rebuke showed their radically different attitudes toward God.

> *You have two choices when you are called out by a prophet: to ignore the call or to recognize the seriousness of your rut.*

Both Saul and David were handsome. "Saul was the most handsome man in Israel—head and shoulders taller than anyone else in the land."[3] Likewise David "was ruddy, with a fine appearance and handsome features."[4]

Both were skilled warriors. Saul's prowess as a warrior was used by God to break down the stronghold of the Philistines.[5] And David was a brilliant military strategist, taking down Israel's enemies one by one.[6]

Both were humble (at least at first). Saul felt so unworthy to take on such a mighty task, he hid when he was chosen by lot to lead.[7] David's father didn't even bother to introduce David to Samuel. As the runt of the litter, David almost missed out on his anointing as king while he was out with the sheep.[8]

But they starkly differed in how they responded to criticism. When God called out Saul for not destroying an enemy army completely, Saul played the victim.[9]

David's response when confronted with his sin stands in stark contrast. "I have sinned against the Lord" is all he said.[10]

Both stumbled in their relationships with God; both committed serious sins that had tragic consequences. *But only David listened to critique.* Saul didn't. David's heart was moved to repent. Saul only made excuses to gain back his title.

The Lyricist

In the ancient world, David was a rock star (literally). And Psalm 51, written following David's encounter with the prophet, contains some of the most vulnerable and honest lyrics I have ever heard:

> Going through the motions doesn't please you,
> a flawless performance is nothing to you.
> I learned God-worship
> when my pride was shattered.
> Heart-shattered lives ready for love
> don't for a moment escape God's notice.[11]

David recognized it wasn't about outward appearances: It wasn't about sacrifices or incense or burnt offerings or religiosity. God wasn't looking for a bribe or excuses. Hearing the prophet, David humbled himself and changed his heart.

David realized that when you encounter a prophet, you have one of two choices: keep plodding in the same direction toward even greater pain or plot a new course.

David needed to change his rut. He needed to repent.

The reputation of the word *repent* has been dragged through the mud of church tradition, and people often associate it with regret, penance, and guilt trips. But all repentance means is *to turn*. Pure and simple. To move in a new direction.

David, more than anyone else, understood that.

People of the Second Chance[12]

Justin and Trisha had a calling. Leaving everything, the young couple moved to Indianapolis in 2002 to start a church for the unchurched. Twelve people attended their first service. But then, things began to go well.

"Freakishly well," said Justin.

Within just one year, they had grown to seven hundred members. In two years, Trisha and Justin were struggling to keep up with the demands. Megachurches had invested resources into the burgeoning church, seeing it as an effective witness in the region. Within three years, Justin had an affair—with the children's church director, who also happened to be Trisha's best friend.[13]

But Justin had been offered a way out.[14]

On a Sunday afternoon several weeks before the affair started, Justin received a call from a board member saying, "Can we go for a drive?"

Driving by a creek, they parked, got out, and sat down on the grass. The board member began pouring out his heart about his marital issues.

Suddenly the Holy Spirit spoke to Justin's spirit, "Justin, you can share your struggles with him. You can share your lust issues with him. You can share your pornography issues with him. This is safe . . . you can be free."[15]

His prophet had spoken. God was offering him an out, but Justin didn't take it. Just when he was about to share, another voice entered his head: "He's your biggest contributor. And it could all end right here."

If Justin was vulnerable, he'd certainly lose a friend. And he'd be fired.

"That was the last time I could really feel the prompting of the Holy Spirit saying, 'You're in dangerous territory,'" said Justin.

Six weeks later, he was having a different conversation. Telling Trisha he no longer wanted to be married to her, Justin confessed that he was having an affair with her best friend.

A New Direction

In the aftermath of the affair—their marriage, family, church destroyed—Justin and Trisha chose a path of reconciliation. They went through months of intense counseling. Trisha said forgiving Justin was the hardest thing she had ever done.

Justin had an even harder time believing that God could use him again. "I had no idea what the future held, but one thing I was sure of: God was done with me," he said.

But that is not the end of the story.

A friend of Justin's sat him down and told him, "God isn't through with you yet."

Together Justin and Trisha fought a painful fight for their marriage. Feeling God calling them to share their story with others, they started RefineUs Ministries four years later, where they began guiding other couples to seek Christ-centered marriages. Justin used to think that mistakes could keep you from using your gifts for God. Today he sees it differently.

"What I have seen is that the more I have sought brokenness, the more opportunity He has given me to live out my calling," he said. "I get cautious when people desire the gifts of God more than they desire brokenness."[16]

Though Justin was going down the wrong rut, he found it is never too late to repent, to restart, to go in another direction.

In his psalm of repentance, David wrote, "What you're after is truth from the inside out. Enter me, then; conceive a new, true life."[17]

New direction. New life. Being reborn. That is true repentance. No longer plodding in the same rut.

Ears to Hear

Shame and embarrassment can make us reluctant to ask for help. We don't want to admit our weaknesses. When we are so focused on doing good, we like pretending we have it all together. But we desperately need to forget our pride and listen to critique in our lives.

Recently, I was criticized for several difficult decisions I had made regarding staffing. An individual scheduled time to meet and then proceeded to detail the reasons I was wrong. As he spoke, my spine stiffened. I found myself preparing my response and the ways I would refute his points.

A series of destructive thoughts raced through my mind: "He doesn't know all the facts. . . . He has no idea the pressure I'm under right now. . . . He's never led an organization like this. . . . He must have some personal agenda. . . ."

But after our unsettling conversation, I had the haunting thought that he just might have spoken truth. I had been so focused on my response that I'd failed to even consider that he might be right.

We are in a dangerous place when we fail to realize that critics often speak a word of truth we need to hear. If we only value positive feedback, over time it becomes easier to surround ourselves with people who agree with us and marginalize those who criticize.

Thinking back to my experience with Greg, my Panera prophet, I'm thankful he provided a wise word at a key moment. I wasn't committing adultery or murder, but I was being

We desperately need to forget our pride and listen to critique in our lives.

foolish. Greg loved me enough to help me understand my own sin—and to once again point me to the message of grace.

He helped me see my need to repent, to change direction. When was the last time you were challenged by a friend, a critic, or even someone you didn't know very well? If you are unable to answer that, it's probably time to seek out coffee with your Panera prophet, and be open to a life-giving critique.

Discussion Questions

1. How do you respond to critique?

2. Do you have a Panera prophet in your life? If so, describe your relationship with this individual.

3. How did you invite this prophet into your life? If you don't currently have a Panera prophet in your life, what are some ways you can invite one to be honest with you?

4. Is the church a place you feel open to share your concerns and struggles, or do you feel like you have to have it all together?

5. How could the church create a place where Christ-followers would feel safe to share about their struggles *before* they self-destruct?

For a video of my Panera prophet Pastor Greg Lafferty discussing having people speak truth into your life, see www.peterkgreer .com/danger/chapter10.

11

WHO AM I WHEN I'M NOT ME?

The Spiritual Danger of Forgetting Your True Identity

Jesus loves me, and that's enough.[1]

—James Mason

Ed Dobson was charismatic. Serving as a megachurch pastor in Grand Rapids, Michigan, for eighteen years, Dobson was named Pastor of the Year by Moody Bible Institute. And it wasn't just a job for Ed—he "loved being a pastor."

He said, "My joy has been to give them a sense of hope." Dobson was constantly interacting with others, being sought for guidance and counsel. He actively served on several prominent nonprofit boards.

After Ed was forced to leave the ministry due to Amyotrophic Lateral Sclerosis (ALS), also known as Lou Gehrig's disease, everything instantaneously changed. The day after he stepped down, his phone stopped ringing. He had his wife call his phone just to make sure it still worked.

No more crowds. No more counseling sessions. It all came to a screeching halt.[2]

Ed's experiences are typical. Losing a job, even through retirement, is a cataclysmic event for most people.

This life-altering transition, unlike any other experience in life, highlights where we find our identity.

Campaign Trail

When I was in graduate school, I heard a veteran congressman share some pretty sobering advice for a roomful of freshman politicians.

At the rooftop luncheon at Harvard's Kennedy School, Congressman Frank Wolf addressed a bipartisan group of incoming congressmen. The excitement in the room was electrifying. Having just experienced the elation of winning a major election, the politicians were giddy. Some had just accomplished a lifelong dream.

But Congressman Wolf shared a startling remark: "Remember who you are, because nothing is dropped faster than a former congressman."

Talk about a downer. They hadn't even settled into their offices, and he was reminding them that the people who were cheering their names would quickly drop them and focus on someone else.

Currently in his seventeenth term in Congress, Congressman Wolf had watched many friends leave Congress, and he knew the exit process was often not graceful. Many of his colleagues decided to cling to their former identities, unable to move on. He wanted these new politicians to remember their current identity was fleeting. And if they didn't remember who they were, when their service ended they'd be left with confusion, emptiness, and a hard landing.

Who Am I?

Before Laurel and I created the guardrails for our marriage that I talked about in chapter 3, I found myself on a plane returning from the Dominican Republic. We'd recently had "the conversation" in which Laurel told me that things couldn't continue like this. With my eyes opened to how I had not prioritized our marriage, I couldn't be halfhearted in addressing our challenges. I needed to be all in.

My hundred plus nights a year away from home conflicted with a healthy home life. On this latest trip, I'd left a family in chaos—Myles, Lili, and Keith all had fevers. Our home toilet wasn't working. Laurel was understandably overwhelmed. Something needed to change.

Due to mechanical problems, I was stranded in transit another day in Florida at a cheap hotel. That evening, I drew up my resume. I reviewed my contacts. I thought it was time for me to transition.

I felt sick about leaving a job I loved. My discontent extended past the fear of being unable to provide: If I quit, my kids would still be able to eat. If I resigned, we'd still have our home. My dissatisfaction even went beyond normal feelings of loss when you leave something you enjoy. For the first time, I recognized that my identity was deeply interwoven with my job.

Nothing is wrong in taking pleasure in your work (Ecclesiastes 3:22). Work is a gift. But finding your identity in your work is a cheap substitute for finding your worth in Jesus Christ.

And I'd forgotten my identity as a Christian *leader* was subordinate to my calling as a *follower* of Him. So wrapped up in doing good things for God, I lost sight of being rooted in Him. So fervent carrying out my work the Lord, I overlooked my obligation to find my identity first as a child of the almighty God.

When I returned home and was able to reconnect with family, it felt like everything had changed. The kids weren't sick anymore; even the day was sunny and bright. Praying about it, Laurel and I together decided that I would stay at the organization. But we also drafted a proposal to my board to cut the number of days of travel I had. God has blessed our marriage and family through this decision.

I love our ministry. And we're planning on staying here for a long time.

But what I *do* is going to change. Perhaps later this year, perhaps a decade down the road. And if I don't know how to describe myself beyond my occupation, I am going to experience a hard landing.

> **"You will be tempted to worship your calling more than you worship Christ."**

Robert Leahy, director of the American Institute for Cognitive Therapy in New York, describes what happens when our identities are wrapped up in what we do: "It's like having your entire investment in one stock, and that stock is your job. You're going to be extremely anxious about losing that job, and depressed if you do."[3]

When we root our identity in the good work we do—whether that's our formal occupation, or our role at church, or our philanthropy, or our time spent serving others through extracurricular activities—we experience another spiritual danger of doing good. We can be so wrapped up in the good we do that as Justin Davis of RefineUs Ministries says, "You will be tempted to worship your calling more than you worship Christ."[4]

A Bad Rap

King David fascinates me. He was a young shepherd boy, anointed by a superstar prophet, and told he would receive a great kingdom. Such a great promise. Such a bright future.

But then he found himself in the wilderness with the outcasts and criminals. His so-called mighty men were nothing more than "losers and vagrants and misfits of all sorts."[5] David was running for his life.

At one point, he was so desperate to escape from Saul that he sought protection from the Philistines—his enemies. When he arrived, the Philistines saw him and recognized him as the slayer of their giant, Goliath. No surprise, they weren't super excited to welcome him to their city.

Realizing this wasn't a bright idea, David decided to act insane so they'd let him go: "So right there, while they were looking at him, he pretended to go crazy, pounding his head on the city gate and foaming at the mouth, spit dripping from his beard."[6]

It doesn't get much worse than standing in front of your enemy, dripping saliva from your mouth and acting like a lunatic.

This was not the high point of David's life.

His identity as warrior extraordinaire, anointed leader of Israel, and childhood prodigy was long gone. But at that moment, David did not cling to his identity as the kid who killed a giant, or the poet, or even a skilled leader.

At one of the lowest points of his life, he wrote Psalm 34,[7] not as a way to complain, but as a song remembering who God is. He wrote, "Taste and see that the Lord is good; blessed is the one who takes refuge in him."[8]

David just pretended to be crazy, everyone seemed to be against him, he thought he was about to die, and he was praising God? He went on to write, "Fear the Lord, you his holy people, for those who fear him lack nothing."[9]

David knew his Father—and that was enough. Yes, he'd lost his reputation. But whether he was slaying a giant or in the heart of his enemies' camp with saliva dripping from his mouth, he was a child of the King.

His identity was firmly established. He knew God saw him as a son and in this position, he lacked nothing.

Likewise, whether we are at the peak of our careers or have just left a position in disgrace, it is comforting to see how David dealt with his identity crisis.

The key is to remember. Remember who God is. Remember His faithfulness. Remember His goodness. Remember His love.

As David said, "Fear the Lord, you his holy people, for those who fear him lack nothing."

Jesus Follower

After Ed Dobson left his full-time pastoral role, he described the feeling of losing his identity.

He said, "It felt like all of a sudden life had come to an end. Life was over. It was like going from 100 miles an hour to zero overnight."[10]

In addition to a radical change in his identity, the doctors had given him only two years to live. That was more than ten years ago.

Faced with his own mortality and his change of position, suddenly Dobson began to seek Scripture in a radically new way. For one year, he studied the life of Jesus and tried to live like Him.

"The paradox is that for me the purpose [of my life at that time] was following Jesus, which I had been trying to do all my life," said Dobson. "Previously I had never had the time to do it."[11]

He no longer speaks to crowds of five thousand and is no longer a full-time "in the pulpit" pastor. Today he meets with people one-on-one. And he says today he listens more than he talks—partly because he doesn't have the answers he once had.

"I know that sounds a bit lame," he said. "I know that I should have all the answers, but the truth is, the more I live, the fewer answers I have."[12]

Many of the people he meets with also have ALS. He says that today though he's no longer preaching and in the ministry spotlight, he has found his true purpose.

> *His identity goes beyond his service and straight to a relationship with his Creator.*

"I am no longer a preacher," said Dobson. "Today, I would say I am a Jesus follower. Period."[13]

His identity goes beyond his service and straight to a relationship with his Creator. This identity is the only one that will last.

Finding Our Vocations

As Ed Dobson discovered, our identity is secure when it is rooted in Jesus. When we truly believe this, the grip our work and service have on our hearts begins to lessen.

What keeps you from cultivating a friendship with your Savior? Busyness? Noise? Unrest? Dobson found that in a fast-paced world, it is work to slow down long enough to listen, to read Scripture, to pray, and to regularly remember *who we are*.

But there's more. Something further keeps us from cultivating an identity rooted in Christ. Author Richard Foster says, "Our busyness seldom keeps us from eating or sleeping or making love."[14] The final barrier is the false belief that we must *do just a little more* before God will love us.

Ironically, it was only when Dobson recognized he didn't have it all together, physically he couldn't do more service, and he didn't have all the right answers that his relationship with Christ grew.

Likewise, if you are still performing for God in some hope that your service will cause God to love you more, you can stop striving. You can let go of your guilt that you haven't done enough. And you can remember that the cross is proof you are a prized child of the King. Stop long enough to taste a divine love that is even better than life.

Discussion Questions

1. Do you spend time with people who don't know (and don't really care) what you do professionally?

2. When you meet people for the first time, how do you describe yourself? Do you lead with what you do or do you lead with your faith and family?

3. Where are some areas that you find your identity?

4. What would it be like for you to take another job? If you're in ministry, would you be willing to take a "normal job," or do you have to be engaged in ministry?

5. What are ways you can better ground your identity in Christ, rather than in your career or through your service?

For a video of Ed Dobson, see www.peterkgreer.com/danger/chapter11.

12

CHRISTIAN KARMA

The Spiritual Danger of Thinking Good Things Always Happen to Good People

God has decided to identify with human beings in all of our human experience. He is not going to be aloof when it comes to relating to people. He is not going to love them from a distance. He is going to go all the way down. He has decided to immerse himself in our discouragement, in our loneliness, in our distraction, in our confusion, in our embarrassment, in whatever we deal with, and to become a part of it.[1]

—Isaac Anderson, Food for the Hungry

Taking my cue from Michael Scott in his mockumentary *The Office*, I sit on the Christmas party committee.

While some dread the annual company Christmas party, I see it as an opportunity to sport my quilted V-neck Christmas sweater and celebrate with a team I count not just as my colleagues, but my close friends.

One year, as the committee gathered to discuss the annual party, our first conversation was regarding our party's theme. Over the past year, God had done the miraculous. Staff at our headquarters overcame cancer. International staff had children healed. After losing our largest donor at a time of national recession, we still grew by over 20 percent. Our theme for the Christmas party was clear: *Miracles.*

Over the year, we had increased the emphasis on prayer throughout the organization—and it seemed as though God was divinely answering each specific prayer. We were praying for God to do abundantly more than we could ask or imagine—and the All Powerful was exceeding our most ambitious prayers.

As part of our Christmas celebration, we were compiling videos from each country celebrating the miracles they experienced throughout the year.

But shortly before the party, the miracles came to a screeching halt and the theme of the party seemed like a cruel joke. One of our dearly loved colleagues and his wife lost a child in late-term pregnancy, despite all our prayers. We were devastated as God remained silent.

It wasn't right. Kevin loved God. He served faithfully. He had made significant sacrifices to join our team. God had just done the miraculous so many times—why didn't the Almighty show up at this moment of need?

Kevin's wife, Lynn, wrote, "If God is a merciful God, why did He forsake us even though we were desperately seeking Him?"

Good people who serve sacrificially should be protected from this sort of pain.

Reading Psalm 23, I was inundated with questions.

The Lord is my shepherd, I shall not want.
Why didn't God heal? Why wasn't the Shepherd watching over His sheep?

He makes me lie down in green pastures; he leads me beside still waters; he restores my soul.

Where is the promised rest and blessing?

He leads me in right paths for his name's sake.

Why can't we even see the right path?

Even though I walk through the darkest valley, I fear no evil; for you are with me; your rod and your staff—they comfort me.

Why do we feel like your rod is being used in punishment instead of in comfort?

You prepare a table before me in the presence of my enemies; you anoint my head with oil; my cup overflows.

Why are people who do not even try to do good protected from these challenges? Why do they flourish while we're in pain?

Surely goodness and mercy shall follow me all the days of my life, and I shall dwell in the house of the Lord my whole life long.[2]

Where are the promised goodness and mercy? Why is this psalm so easy to read when all is going well and so hard to read when we're facing so many challenges?

When God doesn't keep His end of the deal, we wonder how God could even exist. If our kids fall ill, if we experience job loss, or if we go through pain and hardship, then we can feel abandoned. Or we'll feel like we didn't do enough good. Especially in the North American context, affluence has insulated us from a theology of suffering and leaves us open to belief that good people deserve only good things in return for what they've done for God. When we suffer, it seems as if for some unknown reason, God is punishing us.

> **Affluence has insulated us from a theology of suffering and leaves us open to belief that good people deserve only good things.**

It's probably the most painful spiritual danger of doing good, and also the oldest.

Ancient Karma

People think the story of Job is about suffering. Though Job's losses are incredible, the question playing out on earth is, Is God just?

At the heart of the question is a central concept to this spiritual danger of doing good. Beneath the philosophy of Christian karma is the thought, *If God doesn't give us good in return for our good, then is the Good Shepherd really good?*

The common wisdom of the ancient world—as articulated by Job's verbose friends for too many chapters—was also karma. If we do good, then a good God will return the favor. If we do bad, we will be punished. As a righteous man, Job should have been rewarded by God.

But it was (well-disguised) heresy. At the end of it, Job was considered righteous. His friends—whose philosophy was so well articulated—were wrong.

Job was good. God allowed Job to suffer. God is good.

Despite the wisdom of the day, despite what Job's friends believed—God is good.

When Job was vindicated, God said to him, "Pull yourself together, Job! . . . I have some questions for you, and I want some straight answers. Where were you when I created the earth? Tell me, since you know so much!"[3]

Job never found out why he suffered. Most times, we don't either.

Sometimes we see the big picture. Sometimes God reveals to us what He has in mind. Sometimes He doesn't. We simply do not know the ways of God and are left no other option than to trust.

Radical Suffering

If the philosophy of Christian karma were true, then surely some of Jesus' greatest followers would reap the benefits of this philosophy.

But if you look at the disciples, according to tradition, ten of the twelve were martyred. Thomas supposedly was speared to death in India.[4] Philip was stoned to death in modern-day Turkey, his head first fastened to a stake.[5] Brothers Peter and Andrew were both crucified, Peter upside down,[6] and Andrew without being nailed to the cross, but bound—in order to prolong suffering.[7]

God never promised an easy life—and actually promises the opposite: "In this world you will have trouble." However, this sober promise ends with, "But take heart! I have overcome the world."[8]

Painful Prayers

As I write, the past two months have been full of loss. My dad was diagnosed with cancer. My last two living grandparents died. Laurel's dearly loved grandmother with whom she had almost daily conversations since she learned how to use the phone also left this life.

But even these lows that are significant in my life are minor compared to what so many others go through on a daily basis. Traveling around the world, my heart has been broken by the brokenness of the world. I've met godly people who have not experienced a day of health or wealth in their lives, and I know it has nothing to do with the depth of their faith. I question why I receive so many good things in life while mothers fill their children's bellies with sunbaked dirt because it is better than sending their children to bed hungry. It does not seem right that a doctor's report of birth defects or disease shapes the course of a family and determines so much of their lifelong experience. Many times, life just isn't fun in the face of unexplained pain.

I don't know why suffering happens, and trite answers are offensive to those suffering. But I do know what happens when people see the pain of others and respond with Christ's love. In our situation, friends who had been through similar experiences sent us Scripture to focus our minds on the bigger picture. Flowers decorated my dad's hospital room as little reminders of love from around the country. We knew we were not alone. We felt God's presence through the love of others and had times of connection with God we simply don't have when life is without challenge. We longed for Christ's Kingdom to come.

When Kevin and Lynn were going through their pain and when we were in ours, I saw the beauty of people willing to enter the pain of others. The beauty of walking in hard places and in hard circumstances with a God who shows us what love looks like in the midst of pain. Meals delivered. Hospital rooms visited. Homes cleaned.

God doesn't ask us to have all the answers, but simply reminds us that this is not our home. Suffering makes us desperately long for His return and encourages us to follow His example of love in action for those in need.

Christ Suffered With Us

When Christ walked on earth, He was not separated from the brokenness of this world. Instead He entered it.

Christian leader John Stott said, "I could never myself believe in God, if it were not for the cross. . . . In the real world of pain, how could one worship a God who was immune to it?"[9]

Stott shares how he has entered many Buddhist temples while visiting Asian countries and stood respectfully before the Buddha, whose arms are folded and eyes closed, detached from the pain and sorrows of the world.

"But each time after a while I have had to turn away," he said. His imagination would turn to Christ suffering on the cross—"to that lonely, twisted, tortured figure on the cross, nails through hands and feet, back lacerated, limbs wrenched, brow bleeding from thorn-pricks, mouth dry and intolerably thirsty, plunged in God-forsaken darkness. That is the God for me!"[10]

As God entered our brokenness, the Healer is calling you to enter others' pain. He is asking you to identify with your neighbor who may have just lost a job, to fight for the widow and orphan, to value your comfort less than the privilege of comforting others.

Good things don't always happen to good people—but the Good Shepherd is still good and invites you and me to be His hands and feet to those in need, even when we don't have answers to the difficult problem of pain and suffering.

The ultimate miracle worth celebrating at a Christmas party and then living throughout the year is not that God answers a specific prayer for life, health, or strength, but rather that He has given the gift of *Emmanuel*, a God who is with us and for us, even in the midst of unexplained pain.

Discussion Questions

1. Do you see the concept of Christian karma—*if we do good for God, we'll receive blessing from God in return*—evident in the church today?

2. Have you ever bought into the idea of Christian karma? If so, how has this affected your relationship with God?

3. Why is the philosophy of Christian karma a dangerous one to believe?

4. The question at the heart of the Old Testament book of Job is, Is God just? How does this thought relate to Christian karma?

For a video of Tim Keller speaking about pain and suffering, see www.peterkgreer.com/danger/chapter12.

13

SPINACH SALAD WITH A SIDE OF SHAME

The Spiritual Danger of Seeing Everyone's Sin but Your Own

Why do you look at the speck of sawdust in your brother's eye and pay no attention to the plank in your own eye? How can you say to your brother, "Let me take the speck out of your eye," when all the time there is a plank in your own eye? You hypocrite, first take the plank out of your own eye, and then you will see clearly to remove the speck from your brother's eye.[1]

—Jesus

After a full day of meetings in Orange County, California, I was looking forward to dinner. Since arriving in Cali that morning, I had raced nonstop to meetings.

When we arrived at the restaurant, I sat down with my colleague Jenn and several supporters. Trying to be healthier, I ordered a spinach salad. The dinner went as planned: the conversation was engaging, the individuals interested in partnering with our ministry.

Finally, I headed to my hotel, dragging, ready for sleep. But when I looked in the mirror, adrenaline shot through my body. I was wide awake.

A piece of spinach covered my tooth. And it wasn't just a little piece; it was large, ugly, and unmistakable.

As we met for breakfast the next morning, Jenn casually asked, "So, Peter . . . what should I do if you ever . . . oh, I don't know . . . you pray for the wrong person . . . or have something in your teeth?"

I erupted, "You knew about the spinach! And you didn't say anything?" And then I realized the full extent of what she had just said. "And I prayed for the wrong person?" Not a good day.

Supporters had been staring at the hunk of spinach in my teeth, but I hadn't seen it. I was completely unaware. The spinach was ugly.

I can't help but wonder how many other times I've been unable or unwilling to see my own pride, arrogance, selfishness, or other faults—all much more repulsive than just a piece of spinach.

It's possible to challenge supporters to live radically for the poor and then blow money on unnecessary home furnishings.

It's possible to give a talk at a church on God's mercy to the poor and yet be harsh with my own kids when I get home.

It is even possible to give a talk on humility and be proud of how well it is delivered.

The danger of doing good is that I recognize the spinach on your teeth while completely missing it on my own.

Toxic Attitude

I'm a pretty peaceful person, but after I returned from Cambodia, I almost erupted in a grocery store. Having just spent time living in poverty, I entered the store and was overwhelmed by the excess of America. I hit my breaking point in the cereal aisle.

For the past few months in Cambodia, I had eaten the same breakfast every day: leftover rice from the night before with a little bit of milk. My own version of Rice Krispies, albeit an extremely soggy one. It was a special day when I made Cambodian Raisin Bran—aka raisins and sugar added to my leftover mushy rice.

But back in the U.S. grocery store in the cereal aisle with all of its options, I saw a child complaining. Wanting a different type of cereal than her mom was willing to purchase, she was irritated and upset.

I left the aisle before I exploded and committed a misdemeanor with Cocoa Puffs.

Full of self-righteous rage, I stormed out of the grocery store. *People were starving. And she was a selfish, wealthy, and entitled spoiled brat.* My self-righteous indignation extended beyond this one child. I began to blast the North American church for being overfed and uncaring about the needs of the world.

Get Perspective

I gained a new perspective when my friend Jean Marie visited me in my normal, middle-class suburban neighborhood in Lancaster, Pennsylvania. Nice, but nothing fancy. Or so I thought. Jean Marie, a colleague of mine in Burundi, stopped at our house during his visit to the U.S.

I picked him up at the train station. When we arrived at our house, I clicked the button to open the garage door. Jean Marie belly laughed.

"Peter, you're a rich man. You are a rich man," he said to me. "Peter, you are a rich man," he repeated again and again. He got out of the car to inspect the garage-door opener, astonished that we had a machine opening our garage.

Peter, you are a rich man—his words reverberated in my head. Jean Marie was right. I was no Bill Gates, but from a global perspective, I was ridiculously rich. And my "average" life no longer reflected the youthful zeal for the poor I had after returning from Cambodia.

I was in no position to judge the child at the grocery store. In fact, now that I have seen the needs in our world, and yet still daily make decisions that show no regard for the poor and needy, am I not the guilty one? Focusing on the sins of others does no good other than to inflate the ego and increase self-righteousness.

As Christ said, "Take the plank out of your own eye"—before judging people in the cereal aisle.

Sin Hierarchy

I have a "sin ranking," which perhaps not coincidentally enables me to criticize others while feeling pretty good about myself. This is just one more lesson I learned in Rwanda.

Rwanda is a country of captivating beauty with rolling hills and patchwork agriculture. It's where the gorillas really do live in the mist. And it's where examples of forgiveness abound.

But life in Rwanda wasn't always easy.

> *Focusing on the sins of others does no good other than to inflate the ego and increase self-righteousness.*

One morning, I woke up and sensed something was wrong. Like most homes in Kigali, ours had a wall surrounding our property with shards of glass protruding from the top to keep out unwanted visitors. But that morning, disheveled clothes were clumped together on top of the wall. Someone had piled laundry from our neighbors' clothesline to cover the glass and jumped the wall. I rushed into the living room to discover that we had been robbed during the night. I felt violated. Unsafe.

A few months later, our car was broken into while we were in town. The thief took our stereo and all our CDs but left one of his flip-flops. Not a good trade.

Worse, it was around the same time that I had to fire staff members for creatively stealing money. We'd considered them dear friends. We had prayed with them. They had been in our home every Friday night for English club. We had trusted these individuals. We felt betrayed and let down.

I would certainly never steal like *these people*.

Shortly after these thefts, I had a conversation with Rwandese friends who opened my eyes to the sin hierarchy in each culture. My middle-class American lifestyle had taught me that stealing was in the "really bad" sin category. Other cultures felt stealing from a rich foreigner was bad, but not that bad if your family needed to be fed.

They explained that in their sin hierarchy it was appalling that Americans put the elderly in institutions. It was such a form of disrespect that they wondered whether you could truly be a follower of Jesus if you placed your family members in a retirement home. Also, few sins in Rwanda are more reprehensible than getting angry in public. Some Rwandans would wonder whether Americans could follow Jesus Christ and get upset while driving to work.

Following that conversation, I have attempted to focus less on the sins of others and recognize how much work I have to do in my own life. Instead of criticizing others for not doing enough to care for the poor, the orphan, and the widow, I want to get to work loving and serving the most vulnerable. Instead of criticizing others for lavish excess, I want to live much more sacrificially and generously. Instead of criticizing others for hypocrisy, I want to fervently move toward greater authenticity in my own life.

In short, instead of being quick to judge others, I want to emulate Jesus. Looking at His life, I don't see condemnation for anyone except the pious who used religion to lift themselves up while pushing others down. People who came to Jesus to seek mercy found it every time. People who needed forgiveness discovered grace. People who needed healing received wholeness.

Dinner Party

In the Gospels, Jesus was invited to a dinner party. The host was Simon, a religious man. As the festivities went on, the party was disrupted. A woman entered. Not just any woman. She was called a sinful woman. With tears, she wiped Jesus' feet, then kissed them, pouring expensive perfume on them.[2]

Simon was standoffish about the whole thing. Jesus called Simon out. Jesus said to him,

> Do you see this woman? I came into your house. You did not give me any water for my feet, but she wet my feet with her tears and wiped them with her hair. You did not give me a kiss, but this woman, from the time I entered, has not stopped kissing my feet. You did not put oil on my head, but she has poured perfume on my feet.[3]

He went on to say, "Therefore, I tell you, her many sins have been forgiven—as her great love has shown. But whoever has been forgiven little loves little."[4]

I am Simon each time I forget how much I've been forgiven. Loved. Restored.

Like Simon, I've missed out on grace.

Bacardi to Water

Scott Harrison is a hero to me.

Scott used to live the high life. As a nightclub promoter, he was paid two thousand dollars a month just to be seen drinking

Bacardi, was dating a model, and was always hanging out with the rich and famous.

Realizing he was unhappy, Scott left everything to serve overseas for two years, witnessing the suffering of those ravaged by disease and war in West Africa. A changed man, Scott came back to the United States to live here once again.

On his first day back, a friend ordered him a sixteen-dollar margarita. His first inclination was to yell at his friend and tell him that people were dying around the world.

"But I realized guilt was useless," Scott said. Who was he to judge his friend? "This used to be my own life," he said.

Instead of being puffed up with self-righteous anger, he got to work using his many talents in promotion to tell a new story.

> *Because Scott didn't get stuck in his own self-righteous anger, his friends have now been able to share in his new story.*

Scott founded Charity: Water, an organization telling the story of how we can ensure that the world has access to clean water. In the first few years, he raised enough capital to provide clean water to over two million people around the world.

Because Scott didn't get stuck in his own self-righteous anger, his friends have now been able to share in his new story.[5]

Bonfires and Blind Spots

Bonfires lead to candor in conversation like nothing else. After a day of fly fishing, four-wheeling, and male bonding in Colorado with some men further along on the journey than me (aka older), we had a discussion around a fire like one I'd never had before, or since.

Tiger encouraged each of us to share candidly about the others' strengths—but then also to clearly state the blind spots we see in these trusted friends.

With nervous glances, there was an awkward silence as we wondered if we really wanted this sort of transparent feedback.

But after the conversation ended, we each realized the gift it was to have truth spoken in love. Among other comments, they described my youthful idealism and how it can get me in trouble. They spoke about how my belief in other people can cause me to avoid difficult decisions and prolong pain.

While it's not always easy to hear feedback, it was remarkably eye-opening for each of us.

Inviting people to share with you your blind spots may not be easy, but it's worth it: Your friends may tell you about some unwanted spinach in your teeth.

Discussion Questions

1. Have you ever invited someone to share with you your blind spots? If so, discuss.

2. What are situations, actions, and circumstances that cause you to have a strong emotional response? Often these responses stem from our own issues that we project onto others.

3. Why are there different cultural sin hierarchies? How does this play out among people of the same culture who have different experiences and backgrounds?

For a video of Scott Harrison sharing his story, see www.peterkgreer.com/danger/chapter13.

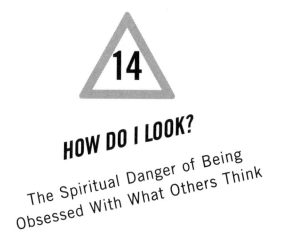

HOW DO I LOOK?

The Spiritual Danger of Being Obsessed With What Others Think

A proud man is always looking down on things and people; and, of course, as long as you are looking down, you cannot see something that is above you.[1]

—C. S. Lewis

While working in microfinance, I was invited to speak at a conference hosted by USAID in Rwanda and Uganda. Fifty microfinance practitioners from all over the world attended this conference hosted at the Hotel Mille Collines. In an attempt to be gracious, at the end of my speech I invited everyone to our offices in Kigali to meet our staff and see the operations firsthand.

In French, I said, "We would welcome you with open arms." Or that's what I thought I said.

Seeing the look of disgust on some of the people's faces, I quickly realized I had made a mistake.

Instead of using the word *bras* (arms), I had accidentally used the word *jambes* (legs). Instead of saying, "We welcome you with open arms," I had said, "We welcome you with open legs." One wrong noun and the invitation had an entirely different—and disturbing—meaning.

After the day was over, I stayed up half the night replaying the look on people's faces—and the shocked response of many reputable people in the field.

It's not the only time I've stayed awake obsessing about what I said, how I performed, and what people thought of me. This ridiculous example has been replayed in other situations in many other ways.

Many people who do good have sleepless nights, wondering, *How did I do? Did people like what I had to say? Did people give me a high rating?*

It's an obsession with impression management—and it's spiritually dangerous. When we're consumed with thinking much of ourselves, we are incapable of thinking much of God.

In the New Testament, Christ recognized that many wouldn't come to Him because "they were more concerned about what people thought of them than about what God thought of them."[2]

Their motivation to do good—to please others—prevented intimacy with God.

Pastor and author Dave Gibbons recently described how a friend prayed over him—in a very loud voice—in the middle of a busy sidewalk in southern California—with people passing by who might know him. After three minutes of this prayer, Dave was ready for it to end. However, after eight minutes, Dave says he heard God whisper, "You are more concerned with what people think of you than with my power."[3]

I can relate.

Am I Doing It Right?

I grew up in a conservative church, and the only time we raised our hands was when we were asking to go to the bathroom.

A few years ago, I found myself in the front row of a contemporary church. I was the guest speaker and was prominently seated right next to the pastor. After a few songs, the worship leader read Psalm 134:2, "Lift up your hands in the sanctuary and praise the Lord."

He reminded the church that raising hands is a natural response to greatness, whether it is an Eagles touchdown or a Manchester United goal. The speaker asked why we wouldn't then raise our hands to celebrate the most incredible victory—the victory over death through the gift of new life in Jesus.

As the songs continued, people in the room began lifting their hands in worship.

Being in the front row, I felt the need to raise my hands as well. But I wanted to get it right. I started wondering, "Do you go with the single hand up or the double? Palms up or down? Arms still or a gentle sway?" I knew I shouldn't copy the pastor, who was dancing with both hands up.

I'm sure I looked like a very confused charismatic as I tried to figure out how to "do it right."

I enjoy a huge variety of worship styles, but the worship of my heart ended the moment I became preoccupied with my hand-raising performance.

More Than Words

Shane Everett of the band Shane and Shane described how the danger to perform for others is even more heightened for the worship leaders themselves. With transparency, he shared that being on stage is "pretty cancerous to the soul. You get a lot of strokes getting on a stage, any kind of stage, whatever that is. Strokes for the believer often create a breeding ground for pride, for less selflessness."[4]

You can be performing for others, trying so hard to look like you're having an experience with God, that you are just having an experience with yourself.

A self-centered preoccupation with our image and performance is further fueled by some of the lyrics we sing. *Worship Leader Magazine* had an article describing how even the lyrics can be all about us.

> Listen next time you're singing in worship. It's about how Jesus forgives me, embraces me, makes me feel his presence, strengthens me, forgives me, holds me close, touches me, revives me, etc., etc. Now this is all fine. But if an extraterrestrial outsider from Mars were to observe us, I think he would say either a) that these people are all mildly dysfunctional and need a lot of hug therapy . . . or b) that they don't give a rip about the rest of the world, that their religion/spirituality makes them as selfish as any nonChristian, but just in spiritual things rather than material ones.[5]

Preoccupation with how we look isn't just an issue confined to how we worship; doing good can be detrimental to our faith any time we perform for the approval of others.

"How do I look?" is a common question to ask, but we don't always want an honest answer. I have a feeling if we really were told by God how we looked, even in moments of great worship and service, we might hear, "You look like a little child trying desperately to gain the approval of people whose opinions don't matter."

A radical, do anything, go anywhere faith can be deeply contaminated by self-love or self-worship.[6]

If only I could preach the perfect sermon. Serve in the most sacrificial way. Win the Nobel Peace Prize. Find myself on a box of Wheaties. Receive a fancy degree from an Ivy League university.

These desires might sound noble, but they might be spiritual heresy because the focus is on ourselves instead of God. The purpose of worship and service is to bring glory to God—the antithesis of selfishness.

We may be doing great things for God, helping others, welcoming people at church, but it is healthy to stop and ask a heart-changing question: "Why are we doing this?" Is it about how it makes us look, or is it in response to undeserved love?

Apples to Oranges

If you grew up in church in the '80s, you might have played the Ungame. It has a board, dice, cards, and looks like a normal game, except there is one major difference: There are no winners and losers. Asking probing questions, it is designed to prompt conversation around a board game that has no distinct starting or ending point.

A radical, do anything, go anywhere faith can be deeply contaminated by self-love or self-worship.

I'm not afraid to admit that I enjoy it, but most of my friends and family can't stand it.

"Why play a game where there's no winner?" my slightly competitive sister-in-law asked on a family vacation.

A naturally competitive person myself, I understand the problem of the Ungame. Winning requires having one person do better than others. It pushes us to perform, to run faster, jump higher, throw further than the other participants.

However, comparison is a dangerous game in faith and is often applied to impression management. As long as we seem to be doing better than others, we must be okay.

We define our good work in comparison to others. I'm not as _____ as _____. Or conversely, I'm better than _____ at _____.

I have my list of rock stars, and Gary Haugen tops the list. He started International Justice Mission the same year as our ministry, and it has experienced much more rapid growth. Brian Fikkert is another all-star—and when he and I launched our first books in 2009, his sold at least ten times as many as mine (and his keeps going). Louie and Shelley Giglio, Jen Hatmaker, Craig Groeschel, Chris Seay, Lecrae, Scott Harrison, Andy Stanley, and David Crowder are all on my list.

While it's good to learn from these rock stars, it's easy for me to become caught up in simply comparing my performance with theirs.

Comparison fuels pride, as C. S. Lewis describes,

Pride gets no pleasure out of having something, only out of having more of it than the next man. . . . It is the comparison that makes you proud: the pleasure of being above the rest. Once the element of competition has gone, pride has gone.[7]

We are not proud because we are intelligent, beautiful, or talented, but because we are smarter, handsomer, or more talented than someone else. Conversely, we're not insecure because of our lack of intelligence but because we don't measure up to our neighbor.

I Don't Care What You Think (I Don't Care What I Think)

In his book *The Freedom of Self-Forgetfulness*, Tim Keller points to the philosophy in vogue today that you overcome approval seeking by refusing to believe what everyone else says about you: Create your own ideals and values.[8] Don't pay attention to anyone else's judgment.

But Paul has another view: "I care very little if I am judged by you or by any human court; indeed, I do not even judge myself.

My conscience is clear, but that does not make me innocent. It is the Lord who judges me."[9]

Disregarding modern philosophy, Paul recognizes that he doesn't get his value from the Corinthians, nor does he get it from himself. He even confesses, "My conscience is clear, but that does not make me innocent." Paul knew he had issues, even calling himself the "worst" of sinners.[10]

> *Paul essentially says, "I don't care what you think; I don't care what I think."*

Instead, Paul essentially says, "I don't care what you think; I don't care what I think."[11]

As Keller writes,

> He refuses to play that game. He does not see a sin and let it destroy his sense of identity. He will not make a connection. Neither does he see an accomplishment and congratulate himself. He sees all kinds of sins in himself—and all kinds of accomplishments too—but he refuses to connect them with himself or his identity. So, although he knows himself to be the chief of sinners, that fact is not going to stop him from doing the thing that he is called to do.[12]

Today God is asking you to stop performing for others so that you can live for your Life-Giver. Let go of trying to "do it right" and instead remember that you are loved because Jesus "did it right." Dressed in His righteousness alone, we will stand faultless before the throne.

When we fully embrace this extraordinary love, we simply don't have time to care so much about what others think.

Discussion Questions

1. Read John 12:42–43. How does wanting approval from others affect those walking with Jesus?

2. Do you see yourself as vulnerable to this particular danger of doing good? Why or why not?

3. In what areas of your life do you compare yourself to others? Is this typically positive or negative?

4. "I don't care what you think. I don't care what I think" sums up Paul's thoughts about impression management. How can this free us from desiring approval?

For a video of worship leader Chuck Gibson talking about the dangers of performance, see www.peterkgreer.com/danger /chapter14.

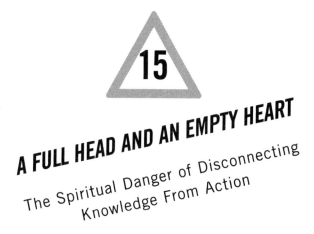

15

A FULL HEAD AND AN EMPTY HEART

The Spiritual Danger of Disconnecting Knowledge From Action

Love the Lord your God with all your heart and with all
your soul and with all your strength.

—Deuteronomy 6:5

While living in Rwanda, I was looking at opportunities to pursue graduate school, and a recruiter from Harvard *just happened* to be stopping in Kigali. How often does that happen?

After my friend Polly introduced us via email, the recruiter and I met at Hotel Mille Collines. At the end of a thirty-minute conversation over coffee in the lobby, he encouraged me to apply. He had never seen my transcript but he mentioned I had a shot at getting in and that there might even be scholarship assistance.

I was blown away by his encouragement and quickly completed my application and essays. However, I still had to score high on the graduate record exam (GRE). Because it was administered at the U.S. Embassy twice a year, I had just one shot to take it before the application deadline.

When the test day arrived, I entered the embassy, sat next to a window, and began to take the test with forty other graduate school hopefuls. Moments later, a jackhammer started to make a deafening sound on the other side of the window. My brain rattled.

"I have to get a good score. I have to get a good score," I mumbled as I attempted to fill in the ovals and block out the demolition. The pressure mounted. My performance plummeted.

To make matters worse, the timekeeper later admitted his watch was broken. He accidentally stopped one of the math sessions ten minutes early.

When the test abruptly ended, I walked out, threw up my hands, and thought, *God, I just royally failed. If you want me to get in, you are going to have to do the miraculous because there is absolutely no way I met the minimum standards.*

Sure enough, I did not meet the standards. My hopes for graduate school were dashed and I once again began exploring Plan B. But several months later, I received a FedEx package from Harvard.

You don't get a FedEx package with a rejection notice. I tore open the package: The first letter said I was accepted. Tucked right behind it was a second letter stating that I had been granted a Public Service Fellowship, a full scholarship—and an annual stipend. Wait. . . . They were literally paying me to go to Harvard?

I'm not an emotional person, but I looked up with tears in my eyes and said, "Thank you."

I'm not sure about God's ways. But from the recruiter being in Kigali to being admitted despite the low score, it's clear God was involved from the start. With absolute certainty I know that the two remarkable years of learning with an incredible group of people in Cambridge was a gift.

I am thankful that the way I got in serves as a constant reminder that I did not do this on my own. It's a small safeguard to the hubris of higher learning.

Today we place a lot of emphasis on education. Our degrees open or close doors. This has spilled over into the church, and we can inadvertently worship our education and our knowledge while forgetting how seldom Jesus seemed to be impressed by the most learned scholars of his time. Our knowledge tends to inflate our egos, while Jesus seems far more concerned about what we are doing with the knowledge we have.

The Good Guys

They were the Bible study leaders. Radical, they would often pray and fast for long periods. Always in church, they could recite Scripture better than anyone. Yet, they somehow ended up receiving the harshest criticism from Jesus.

The Pharisees demonstrate how easy it is to become educated beyond our obedience. With unparalleled head knowledge, they failed to live a life of love.

The Pharisees believed their nation had turned its back on God—and they were ready to bring it back. As the spiritual architects focused on rebuilding the soul of a nation, they followed the prophet Ezra, who "had devoted himself to the study and observance of the Law of the Lord, and to teaching its decrees and laws in Israel."[1]

Zealous for God, they sought to apply their faith to all realms of life. Even though they were a small minority of the population, they exercised a disproportionate influence on the nation.

By separating themselves through rigorous study, distinctive dress, and complete adherence to the moral code, they made sure that everyone knew they were "the faithful." Fervently loyal to God, they dedicated themselves to the study of Scripture and memorized massive sections. They were the few, the proud, the Pharisees.

Despite their whole-life commitment to holiness and unmatched knowledge, John the Baptist called them a "brood of vipers."[2] Jesus continued the criticism by calling them "whitewashed tombs"[3] and rebuked them by saying, "You snakes! You brood of vipers! How will you escape being condemned to hell?"[4]

How did this group who knew Scripture better than anyone else get it so wrong? In knowing all the right answers, the experts in the law "load[ed] people down with burdens they can hardly carry, and you yourselves will not lift one finger to help them."[5]

Jesus clearly stated that head knowledge just isn't enough.

Head, Heart, and Hands

Dennis Hollinger, a friend and president of Gordon-Conwell Theological Seminary, wrote a book titled *Head, Heart and Hands: Bringing Together Christian Thought, Passion and Action.* He says that *faith of the head* is alive in individuals interested in sound theology and those with a firm grasp of apologetics. *Faith of the heart* appeals to individuals who often experience faith in a mystical and emotional sense, and it lends itself to contemplation and meditative practices. *Faith of the hands* fascinates those who are doers, people interested in carrying out works of justice. He argues that each is necessary, and we are a lopsided church when we get these three aspects of expressing our faith out of balance.

A focus on "doing" without an emphasis on learning has no solid foundation. So I'm thankful for those who are scholars, theologians, and teachers, helping us to more clearly understand God and dig into Scripture. Scripture comes alive and takes on much greater meaning when we grow in understanding its original context.

But even today, biblical scholarship and head knowledge of Scripture can create obstacles to the Gospel.

On a Tuesday evening, I was asked to present our organization's work to a church's mission team. We were expanding into a closed country in Central Asia and given their outreach emphasis, they seemed like an ideal partner.

> *Biblical scholarship and head knowledge of Scripture can create obstacles to the Gospel.*

The meeting went well until they began pushing me on our ministry's eschatology (beliefs about the end times).

I was surprised—and couldn't help but think about the country where we served, which had less than 1 percent of the population following Jesus. I wondered if this was the key issue we should emphasize as we sought to bring the message of Jesus to this closed context. We were aligned in all other aspects of the ministry.

Walking out of the church, I left without a partnership, but with two thoughts.

First, these were some of the brightest and most doctrinally sound people I'd ever met. And second, though I appreciated their commitment to doctrine, they seemed to miss the big picture.

They were unwilling to partner with any organization that was not doctrinally aligned with them 100 percent. (As you can guess, they gave to very few ministries.)

Their preoccupation kept them from giving and showing love in a country that desperately needed to see love. It kept them from impacting a world in need.

The Know-It-All Who Gave It All Away

Jesus could have been the ultimate know-it-all. As the Son of God, He had every right to use His spiritual knowledge as a weapon to

God uses the unexpected, the unimpressive, and the lowly to do His Kingdom work.

gain power. But Jesus understood that truth's purpose is to point people to grace.[6] Without sacrifice, without love, knowledge is empty.

But sometimes the church has had a hard time putting this into practice.

Take the church in Corinth. Worldly, the Corinthians were educated and considered themselves wise, spiritually mature.[7]

But Paul deflated their egos. He told them, *God didn't choose you because of your theological prowess; rather it was because you weren't all that impressive.* God uses the unexpected, the unimpressive, and the lowly to do His Kingdom work.

Paul told them:

> But God chose the foolish things of the world to shame the wise; God chose the weak things of the world to shame the strong. God chose the lowly things of this world and the despised things—and the things that are not—to nullify the things that are, so that no one may boast before him.[8]

The Right Mix

Instead of being spiritually arrogant, let's remember that you and I are unlikely choices to carry out Kingdom work. We can stop pretending we have all the answers and leave room for mystery and wonder.

A full head without a full heart is dangerous to the faith. We get to avoid this spiritual danger by entering a grand new story: one where increased knowledge and depth of insight lead to a life of greater love, giving, and sacrifice.

Discussion Questions

1. We often focus on one of the following components of our faith over the others: head (knowledge), heart (emotion),

or hands (action). How do you most naturally express your faith?

2. What would happen if a community of believers focused on one expression of faith over another?

3. God uses unlikely people and unexpected ways to bring about His Kingdom. How have you seen God use you in unlikely ways?

To hear Dr. Hollinger share about *Head, Heart and Hands*, see www.peterkgreer.com/danger/chapter15.

16

MAN MAKEUP

The Spiritual Danger of Pretending to Have It All Together

Pride makes us artificial and humility makes us real.

—Thomas Merton

During a leadership conference last spring, I was invited backstage into the speakers' room. They had toasted almonds (which were amazing), beverages, and several television screens broadcasting sessions. After a final handful of almonds, I left the room, rounded the corner, and recognized one of the featured speakers talking on his phone in the hallway.

To make it appear as if I were accustomed to being backstage, I nonchalantly continued toward him. The closer I got to him, the more I realized he looked different than he had on stage just moments earlier. Something just didn't look right, but I could not put my finger on why.

Then it clicked: man makeup. Yes, he was most certainly wearing man makeup. *A lot* of man makeup. That golden brown tan wasn't from weekend sailing trips. It was bronzer. Caught off guard, I tried not to stare.

Man makeup isn't just something we apply to our faces at speaking engagements. When we are attempting to be seen as do-gooders, we aren't supposed to have any blemishes that could tarnish our golden reputations. We desperately try to appear as if we have it all together. For most, makeup is not an optional piece of the wardrobe; it's a necessity. (And just for the record, I would gladly wear man makeup for another handful of toasted almonds or a speaking opportunity.)

It's easy to apply a little more makeup to undesirable parts of our lives. While few are on the main stage, it's simple to be made up for those watching us every day—to create an outward image completely different from the people we know ourselves to be. The gulf between who others think we are and who we know we are widens. While it's unnatural to wear copious amounts of cover-up on our faces, it's toxic to pretend we have it all together.

Jesus called out the religious for wearing makeup. He said they were "whitewashed tombs."[1] On the outside they looked good, but there was a chasm between their outward appearances and their hearts. They were dead on the inside.

Chemical Makeup

Cambodia was the first country where I served internationally. On my first day in Phnom Penh, the capital, I wanted to fit in. Given an address for the headquarters, I hopped on my moped and made my way through the streets amid the busy marketplace. What I didn't know was that the hand brake was broken.

The dense traffic was stopping at a red light. Going 30 miles per hour, I needed to stop—quickly—and so I desperately pressed on the hand brake. I didn't slow down. I tried to pull a Fred Flintstone with my feet, but as I put my feet on the ground, I lost control. *Smack.* I slammed into a fruit vendor, fell off my moped, and ungracefully sprawled on the ground. Fruit splattered. My hands and knees oozed red.

But I didn't notice. The only thing going through my mind as I jumped up was *Who saw me?* I didn't care if I had broken bones or a bloody shirt. I only wanted to minimize who saw me have such an absurd crash. (Sad to say, a crowd had gathered to watch the ridiculous foreigner who clearly didn't know how to drive a moped.)

That's how I'm wired—and it seems many others who do good are wired a similar way. We want to keep things looking good on the outside no matter how much pain we might be in.

Although I quickly healed from the crash, it will take much longer to heal from the spiritual danger of focusing on external appearances instead of the condition of my heart. I still want to hide my flaws. I still want to pretend I have it all together. I still want to be liked.

A dangerous lie grips my mind: If I wear makeup—and hide my flaws—then my mission will flourish. If people knew my struggles, they wouldn't like me or the ministry as much.

I tell myself: *I'm doing it for the mission of Christ.* But that is inauthentic, a false presentation that undermines the life-transforming message of the Gospel.

The Church With the Man Makeup

God isn't interested in a church pretending to have it all together. Consider Laodicea, one of the seven churches mentioned in the book of Revelation.

More than any other church, *Laodicea was positioned to have maximum impact.*

It was affluent. The city of Laodicea was a merchant banking center, so the church had the resources to effect change. *It had human capacity.* The congregation was filled with talented and engaging people. Nearby was a famous medical school, and it was also a hot spot for entrepreneurs. (Laodicea was famous for its garment trade.) *It was culturally relevant.* Positioned along the trade routes, Laodicea was an epicenter for the exchange of cultural ideas.

> **A dangerous lie grips my mind: If I wear makeup—and hide my flaws—then my mission will flourish.**

Yet something was wrong.

The city did have one major flaw: its water. At the ruins, you can still see the calcified pipes from the water system. Laodicea had warm water with high mineral content. The people had to deal with lukewarm water that probably tasted like nickel.

Jesus used this as a metaphor for the church. On the outside, the church at Laodicea had everything going for it. But Jesus saw that their insides didn't match their healthy exterior.

Jesus said, "So, because you are lukewarm—neither hot nor cold—I am about to spit you out of my mouth."[2]

When Jesus says "spit you out," what He is saying is "vomit." Churches and people who pretend to have it all together make God want to vomit.

Wash It Off

Several years ago, before Laurel and I hit our low point, a man came to me and poured out his heart about his marital issues.

Instead of admitting I had just as many problems, I sat and listened. But the worst part was that I then offered marital advice.

Looking back, I should have heeded the proverb, "Physician, heal yourself!" I preferred to pretend I had it all together instead of opening up that my marriage was in a similar place—that I needed help just as badly as he did. I did my friend and myself a disservice. I'm beginning to see the freedom that comes when I can stop pretending I have it all together (because I clearly don't!). And if you spend time with me, you will continue to see areas where I keep falling into the spiritual dangers described in this book:

- Though I recognize the danger in acknowledging everyone else's sin but my own, I still judge others while being blind to my own faults.

- Though I recognize the danger of ministry becoming my mistress, I still easily become preoccupied with that extra project and miss key family events.

- Though I know in my head that our culture has often adopted the wrong idea of success, I still have a difficult time not becoming obsessed with growth rates.

- Though I know how critical it is to have 3 a.m. friends, I still don't make them a priority.

- Though I know suffering provides an opportunity to serve others, I still miss opportunities to show up.

- Though I know the sacred/secular divide is rubbish, I still elevate ministry and service above the beauty of a church fully involved in serving Christ in all realms of society.

- Though I know the importance of inviting prophetic critique into my life, I still prefer people to tell me what I want to hear.

And the list goes on.

If you are a person who sees the spiritual dangers of doing good, the good news is God already knows you don't have it all together. You haven't earned a gift of grace. He's given it to you. You just have to recognize you're messed up. You get to stop pretending.

Admitting "I'm messed up" is probably one of the most freeing things I've ever done. Confessing we don't have it all together also empowers the body of Christ. Musician Thad Cockrell said, "Strengths divide, but faults unite."[3]

There is something beautiful when we take off the mask: *Our mutual brokenness brings us together.* We can care for one another, showing true compassion toward each other in our weaknesses and strengthening each other to fight to live for Christ.

So how do we deal with the ugly face beneath the makeup?

We have two choices: (1) Keep up the show and pretend we have it all together or (2) Be more honest about the fact that we're a mess.

In an attempt to wash off the man makeup, Mike Foster did an experiment and encouraged people to post pictures taken right after they woke up. Before a shower. Before makeup. Before any sort of cream or gel or toothpaste. The collection of photos shows bedheads and pimples. While you're at it, post a picture of your kitchen when the dishes aren't washed and the floor is stained with breakfast. Go ahead and take a risk in showing people you don't have it all together. My guess is you will hear a collective sigh of relief from others who desperately want to stop believing that everyone else is always beautiful.

In the Old Testament, David regularly asked God to "search" and "test" his heart to see "if there is any offensive way" in him.[4] He wanted God to burst his polished exterior and open his eyes to his own sinfulness.

> **When you and I stop pretending, we come much closer to a point of healing and restoration.**

When you and I stop pretending, we come much closer to a point of healing and restoration.

If, after a heart checkup, we find we aren't who others think we are, or our relationship with God is lukewarm, the good news is God has an incredible offer for us. He extends to us the same offer He gave to Laodicea: "Here I am! I stand at the door and knock. If anyone hears my voice and opens the door, I will come in and eat with that person, and they with me."[5]

It's time to open the door and stop pretending. It's time to admit we have a messy kitchen and an even messier heart. Jesus is waiting to step into our ruin, our shame, our secrets, and our flaws and bring comfort to the hurting, hope to the depressed, and acceptance to the humiliated.

You are loved just as you are.

Discussion Questions

1. What are some of the reasons we wear "man makeup," or put up a front that says we have it all together?

2. How do we foster openness? How can we better handle the grit and mess of everyday life?

3. How has a weakness or struggle in your life led to a greater dependence on God?

To hear a talk I gave on Laodicea and the modern church, see www.peterkgreer.com/danger/chapter16.

YOU-TURN

Compared to the high privilege of knowing Christ Jesus as my Master, firsthand, everything I once thought I had going for me is insignificant—dog dung.[1]

—Paul

In my junior year of college, I spent a summer living with the Amiards, a very special French family, in their home near the Arc de Triomphe in Paris. Evenings were spent meandering down the elegance of the lighted Champs-Élysées to Le Louvre. Days were spent exploring Musée d'Orsay and walking around Notre Dame. But after frequenting the hot spots, I found even more joy in discovering the less popular local sites. Doing my best to blend in with the Parisians, I tried to lose my American accent and the tourist giveaway sneakers.

I thought I'd mastered life as a Parisian, but a trip with my family showed how little I knew. At the end of the summer, my American family visited. Proud of my newly acquired European sophistication, I wanted to be the perfect tour guide. Parading my parents and siblings around Paris on the Metro, all went well. Then it was time to go to the countryside to visit a missionary family near the border of Switzerland.

Chauffeuring my family to the Gare du Nord train station, I showed off my French skills as I bought tickets for everyone. The train was set to leave in twenty minutes. As my family settled into their seats, I set out to the train station's bakery to buy baguettes for the journey, playing my role as the ever-attentive host.

Inhaling the freshly baked bread as I stopped to pay, suddenly I saw the train start moving. Grabbing the bread, I ran and boarded the train just as it picked up speed and the doors locked. I sighed in relief. I had barely made it.

Looking around, I noticed my family wasn't in the car I boarded. I walked onto the next car. Neither were they there. Car after car, I walked through until I realized I was alone and on the wrong train. I had no passport. I had no phone. It was just me and my bag of baguettes.

When I finally met the conductor, I frantically asked where the train was heading. "Dijon" was his response—a very different city from where my family was going on another train.

With a feeling of panic rising in my chest, I shouted, "Arrêtez le train! Arrêtez le train!" ("Stop the train!")

He looked at me and said, "Non, non, non . . ." as he waved his finger in my face. The doors were locked. Like a stowaway, I was placed in the baggage department feeling very silly and very sorry for myself until the train arrived in Dijon.

Eventually, after realizing I was a lost and foolish American college student rather than someone trying to get a free ride, the conductor had pity on me. He notified the train authority. They made an announcement over the loud speaker at the train station where my family was frantically waiting. The conductor let me watch soccer with him at the Dijon train station, and then put me on the next train to meet up with my anxiously waiting family. Soon enough, we were enjoying our vacation once again.

Remembering the incident, I am struck by how thoroughly persuaded I was that I was on the right train. I thought I was an experienced Parisian and was overconfident in my abilities.

It's amazing how you can be convinced you are headed in the right direction—but be on the wrong train.

In this book, we explored several specific spiritual dangers of doing good. If you discover you are serving in the wrong way, it is possible to change direction and rediscover the heart of genuine service.

Unbound

There once was a very good man who also thought he was heading in the right direction. He was from the right family. Dignified and successful, he studied at the best institutions and was marked for success. His name was Saul.

God gave Saul a powerful wake-up call, perhaps because nothing else would have gotten his attention—he was so thoroughly convinced he was on the right road.

It's amazing how you can be convinced you are headed in the right direction—but be on the wrong train.

Blinded on the road to Damascus by Christ, a self-reliant Saul had to ask for help. In order for Saul to become of use to the cause of Christ, he had to realize his desperate need for an undeserved gift.

God has a reputation of using people who are gloriously aware of their inadequacies; from Mary to the disciples to David to Paul . . . the list goes on and on. God has a pattern of humbling the mighty and lifting the humble.

This is really good news for me as I come to an understanding of how my own selfishness impacts even my service and ministry. It's a sign of health when we recognize and begin to grieve that even our most glorious moments of service are tainted by selfish motives.

But the change from Saul to Paul wasn't easy. We sometimes miss that. Even after his dramatic conversion on the road to Damascus, Paul struggled with his selfishness, pride, and sin. Calling himself the "worst" of sinners,[2] he also realized that although God forgives us by His grace, we still need to discipline ourselves.

Sin is a lifelong struggle. Paul later wrote to the Corinthians that "I strike a blow to my body and make it my slave so that after I have preached to others, I myself will not be disqualified for the prize."[3]

Paul fought to live fully for Christ—and you and I have to as well. There are no shortcuts. No three easy steps. Few complete victories.

Philosopher Dallas Willard shares what it's like to grapple with discipleship today:

> We are saved by grace, of course, and by it alone, and not because we deserve it. That is the basis of God's acceptance of us. But grace does *not* mean that sufficient strength and insight will be automatically "infused" into our being in the moment of need. . . . A baseball player who expects to excel in the game without adequate exercise of his body is no more ridiculous than the Christian who hopes to be able to act in the manner of Christ when put to the test without the appropriate exercise in godly living.[4]

This is a battle. To return to Proverbs, "Above all else, guard your heart, for it is the wellspring of life."[5] Prayer, worship, meditation, Scripture memory, and fasting are all part of nurturing the inner life of our hearts so that we can continue to live well.

More than anything else, though, we must remember this—good things apart from God are a threat to knowing our Creator.

Without God, we can do *nothing*. Our power isn't enough. Our talents aren't enough. And our intelligence is insufficient too.

But in this upside-down Kingdom, we find strength through our weakness: "But he said to me, 'My grace is sufficient for you, for my power is made perfect in weakness.' Therefore I will boast all the more gladly about my weaknesses, so that Christ's power may rest on me."[6]

We can strive. We can even make progress against the insidiousness of pride and selfishness in our lives. But ultimately, the only cure is what Christ has already done. "Jesus paid it all, all to Him I owe."[7]

Paul's solution to the struggle is yours and mine as well: "Thanks be to God, who delivers me through Jesus Christ our Lord!"[8]

Good things apart from God are a threat to knowing our Creator.

It's because of this cosmic act of forgiveness that we find the desire to keep pursuing godliness and righteousness.

Tim Keller writes, "Without a knowledge of our extreme sin, payment of the cross seems trivial and does not electrify or transform."[9]

Seeing the depth of my own sin, I feel all the more gratitude for what Christ has done.

For those who are forgiven much, love much.[10]

Father of Modern Missions

J. Hudson Taylor was a young and passionate Christ-follower. At twenty-one years old, he set out from England to China to share the message of the Gospel.

Hudson was extremely talented: He had great intellect, wrote well, was a doctor, and could persuade others to join his cause. With natural charisma and personal charm, he spoke at rallies and convinced many of the importance of the mission field in China.

But upon returning to China for the second time in 1866, he was burned out and spiritually bankrupt. Several tragedies took place. His daughter Gracie died. And after bringing in many new missionaries, their compound was attacked, robbed, and much of it burned. Back in England, people started gossiping about Hudson and the other missionaries—they were seen as crazy, lunatics. Support started draining away.[11]

Depressed, Hudson hit rock bottom. Almost at the point of suicide, he received a note from his friend. As Hudson wrote:

> When my agony of soul was at its height, a sentence in a letter from dear McCarthy was used to remove the scales from my eyes, and the Spirit of God revealed to me the truth of our *oneness with Jesus* as I had never known it before. . . .
>
> "But how to get faith strengthened? Not by striving after faith, but by resting on the Faithful One."[12]

At that point, he thought, "I have striven in vain to rest in Him. I'll strive no more. For has not *He* promised to abide with me—never to leave me, never to fail me?"[13]

This letter changed his life. He later called the period afterward the "exchanged life." He realized even if he didn't have it all together, God did. Though his life saw many more obstacles, Hudson no longer battled them in his own strength. Instead he sought to give it all up to Christ.

Hudson, rejuvenated, continued to carry out the message of the Gospel in China, and by 1895, 641 missionaries were working with his mission agency.[14] When he died in 1905, God had used China Inland Mission to develop "a witnessing Chinese church of 125,000."[15]

"There are not two Christs—an easy-going one for easy-going Christians, and a suffering, toiling one for exceptional believers," Taylor said. "There is only one Christ. Are you willing to abide in Him, and thus to bear much fruit?"[16]

Today we see the "fruit" of Hudson's life.

Despite being a formally atheist nation, China is now home to a growing and dynamic church. One in three Chinese now consider themselves religious.[17] The dynamic heritage of the Chinese church reflects the man who dedicated his life to bringing the Good News to China.

The Comeback Church

We need to celebrate comeback stories in our church today. With so much brokenness and so many dangers, we want to celebrate stories of people who don't have it all together, who are broken, messed up, but come back with a renewed reliance on God's grace.

These are the Comeback Kids: former do-gooders who are becoming ever more aware of their sin and as a result, totally dependent on God's deep grace in their lives. And it's through these people, those like Paul and Hudson Taylor, that Jesus changes the world.

Discussion Questions

1. Doing good things apart from God is a spiritual threat to a growing relationship with Him. Have you seen examples of this in your own life?

2. Read 2 Corinthians 12:6–10. Why did Paul boast in his weakness? What can Paul's thoughts teach us about growing in our faith?

3. How can we celebrate comeback stories in the church today?

To hear Dallas Willard speak about discipleship, see www .peterkgreer.com/danger/chapter17.

CONCLUSION

At a lodge an hour outside Manhattan, twelve of the most promising and talented social entrepreneurs gathered for a weekend of coaching and mentoring, part of a year-long fellowship called Praxis, a Christ-centered social incubator. With the backdrop of rugged cliffs and autumn colors, leaders joined to breathe in the crisp air and to become better equipped to solve the world's greatest problems.

A remarkable group of faith-infused next-generation leaders, the Praxis Fellows immediately impressed me. Enthusiastic, they are ready to change the world. All are putting their faith into action. Most of these leaders are under thirty. They are dedicated. Gifted. Driven.

Inspired by them, I want to celebrate their world-changing work and encourage them to do even more.

Although I was asked to share with them about strategy, funding, and organizational sustainability, I could not help going off topic. I couldn't shake my belief that their greatest danger doesn't lie in organizational design or operational issues. Rather, their greatest danger is hidden in their own hearts.

Two thousand years ago, the ancient province of Judea faced many external threats: brutal rule from a foreign empire, political and religious turmoil throughout the state. When Jesus walked on earth, He could have addressed these huge issues.

Instead, Jesus asked them to first look at themselves. He said, "For it is from *within*, out of a person's heart, that evil thoughts come."[1]

Humanity hasn't changed much since. The greatest danger comes from within. As I shared with the Praxis members, I found myself compelled to speak about not only strategic planning, but the need to protect themselves from their own success and their service—*from the spiritual dangers of doing good.*

We can't live well on our own. Unless I have 3 a.m. friends, unless I surround myself with people willing to tell me the truth I don't want to hear, unless I constantly reflect on my sin and my Savior's love and forgiveness, I am just as capable of royally messing up as anyone else.

At the same time, even if I create lists of precautions, they are just that—guidelines and precautions. At the core, we still need the Holy Spirit to guide us, to open our hearts, to convict us of our sins, and to whisper reminders to us that doing good isn't going to make God love us more than He already does.

Throughout this book, we've spent a lot of time looking at the specific dangers of doing good. My message to Christ-followers like those at Praxis, to people who want to go beyond a lukewarm faith, to people who desire to serve and to live out Isaiah 58, to *you*, is this: Let's not tire of doing good.

But let's remember why we serve. It's not to gain leverage over God. It's not for the purpose of making a name for ourselves or creating a successful organization. It's out of a heart posture of gratitude to a God who knows we aren't perfect, who recognizes that we are a mess, and who loves us anyway.

Ultimately, it's simply a response to the most radical generosity the world has ever known.

NOTES

Foreword

1. Romans 7:21
2. Ephesians 2:6 NIV 1984
3. Romans 8:7
4. Galatians 5:17
5. Romans 7:24–25

Introduction

1. I highly recommend Bob Lupton's book *Toxic Charity* and Steve Corbett and Brian Fikkert's book *When Helping Hurts*.

2. In the early '90s Fuller Seminary professor Dr. J. Robert Clinton did a study finding only one in three biblical leaders finished well; he estimates less than one in three finish well today. Dr. J. Robert Clinton, "Finishing Well—Six Characteristics," http://garyrohrmayer.typepad.com/files/3finishwellarticles.pdf.

3. Proverbs 4:23 NIV 1984

Chapter 1: Confessions of a Do-Gooder

1. Matthew 6:1–4 THE MESSAGE

Chapter 2: Sparky Grace

1. Psalm 51:16–17 THE MESSAGE
2. Tim Keller, *The Prodigal God* (New York: Penguin, 2008), 9.

3. Luke 15:28 THE MESSAGE

4. Luke 15:28–32 THE MESSAGE

5. Eugene Peterson, "Spirituality for All the Wrong Reasons," *Christianity Today*, March 2005, 45.

6. Philip Yancey, *What's So Amazing About Grace?* (Grand Rapids, MI: Zondervan, 1997), 198.

Chapter 3: When Ministry Becomes Your Mistress

1. Marc Lallanilla, "Vitamins: Too Much of a Good Thing?" ABC News, February 23, 2012, http://abcnews.go.com/Health/Technology/story?id=118252&page=1#.T95jBVJhOSq.

2. Ibid.

3. Tim Stafford, "Imperfect Instrument," *Christianity Today*, March 2005, www.christianitytoday.com/ct/2005/march/19.56.html.

4. Thomas A. Powell Sr., "Forced Terminations Among Clergy: Causes and Recovery," Liberty Baptist Theological Seminary, September 2008, http://digitalcommons.liberty.edu/cgi/viewcontent.cgi?article=1171&context=doctoral.

5. To my single friends, I wondered about including this chapter because it could unintentionally reinforce the too prevalent notion that everyone is supposed to be married and that in some way you're "incomplete" until you find that special someone. That thinking and pressure is based on a warped Christian subculture and not Scripture.

6. Matthew 15:3–5 THE MESSAGE

7. "What Did Jesus Mean in Matthew 15 and Mark 7?" *Jesus' Words Only*, www.jesuswordsonly.com/component/content/article/13-background-jwos/230-korban-or-corban-jesus-criticized.html.

8. Exodus 20:12

9. Wayne Jackson, "What Is the Meaning of 'Corban'?" *Christian Courier*, www.christiancourier.com/articles/1086-what-is-the-meaning-of-corban.

10. Tod Kennedy, "Matthew Chapter 15, Wash Hands," *Spokane Bible Church*, April–May 2007, www.spokanebiblechurch.com/study/Matthew/Matthew15.htm.

11. Matthew 15:6–7, 10–11 THE MESSAGE

12. If one or more family members travel with me, it does not count toward this monthly goal. We've created some very special family memories traveling together.

Chapter 4: Stuck in a Rut

1. John 15:5
2. See Matthew 7:22–23
3. John 15:5
4. Thanks to my friend Don Eberly for this insight.
5. Romans 5:8
6. John 3:16
7. Jeremiah 17:9

Chapter 5: Silverbacks and Small Steps

1. Proverbs 16:25
2. Wayde Goodall, *Why Great Men Fall* (Green Forest, AR: New Leaf Press, 2006), 26.
3. Ibid., 136.
4. After researching the Rwandan labor code, we determined it was more appropriate to allow them to sign their own resignation letters than to fire them.
5. 2 Samuel 11:1, italics mine.
6. I heard Andy Stanley use a similar group of questions in a talk.
7. Matthew 15:19–20, italics mine.
8. Andy Court, Kevin Livelli, and Maria Usman, "Questions over Greg Mortenson's Stories," *60 Minutes, CBS*, April 15, 2011, accessed August 22, 2012, www.cbsnews.com/stories/2011/04/15/60minutes/main20054397 .shtml.
9. Alex Heard, "Greg Mortenson Speaks: The embattled director of the Central Asia Institute responds to allegations of financial mismanagement and that he fabricated stories in his bestselling book Three Cups of Tea," *Outside* Magazine, accessed August 15, 2012, www.outsideonline.com/ outdoor-adventure/Greg-Mortenson-Speaks.html?page=2.
10. Ibid.
11. *The Reliable Source* (Roxanne Roberts and Amy Argetsinger, columnists), "Update: Jon Krakauer slams Greg Mortenson in digital exposé," *The Washington Post Blog,* April 19, 2011, accessed August 22, 2012, www. washingtonpost.com/blogs/reliable-source/post/jon-krakauer-slams-greg-mortenson-in-digital-expose/2011/04/19/AFxToE6D_blog.html.
12. *The Reliable Source* (Roxanne Roberts and Amy Argetsinger, columnists), "Update: Greg Mortenson to repay Central Asia Institute," *The Washington Post Blog*, April 5, 2012, accessed August 22, 2012, www.washingtonpost.com/blogs/reliable-source/post/update-greg

-mortenson-to-repay-central-asia-institute/2012/04/05/gIQAgSd8xS_blog
.html.

13. Thomas A. Powell Sr., "Forced Terminations Among Clergy: Causes and Recovery," Liberty Baptist Theological Seminary, September 2008, http://digitalcommons.liberty.edu/cgi/viewcontent.cgi?article=1171&context=doctoral.

14. Psalm 119:10–11

Chapter 6: What Goes Up

1. Simon Robinson and Vivienne Walt, "The Deadliest War in the World," May 28, 2006, www.time.com/time/magazine/article/0,9171, 1198921,00.html#ixzz2GydIXcbz.

2. Fiona Lloyd-Davies, "Why eastern DR Congo is 'rape capital of the world,'" CNN, November 5, 2011, www.cnn.com/2011/11/24/world/africa/democratic-congo-rape/index.html.

3. 2 Samuel 7:3

4. I am indebted to Ryan Rasmussen for coining this phrase in "Confessions of a Proud Pastor," *Relevant Magazine*, October 3, 2012, www.relevantmagazine.com/god/church/confessions-proud-pastor.

5. Proverbs 16:18

6. Paul J. Griffiths, *Lying: Augustinian Theology of Duplicity* (Grand Rapids, MI: Brazos Press, 2004), 60.

7. Ibid., 55.

8. Richard Foster, *The Challenge of the Disciplined Life: Christian Reflections on Money, Sex & Power* (San Francisco: Harper & Row, 1985), 219.

9. Jeremiah 16:2, 5–9

10. Jeremiah 20:7

11. Jeremiah 11:18–23

12. Jeremiah 20:1–2; 38–39

13. Jeremiah 42–43:7

14. "Doing Business in the New Normal" Entrepreneur's Conference in Duluth, Georgia. October 23, 2012.

15. Devotional given at the Reynolds Plantation in Georgia, October 21, 2012.

16. Matthew 23:6–7

Chapter 7: 3 A.M. Friends

1. Dave is a fictitious name, and some details have been changed.

2. Brian is a fictitious name, and some details have been changed.

3. Matthew 14:25 NLT

4. Mark 6:47–48

5. Thomas A. Powell Sr., "Forced Terminations Among Clergy: Causes and Recovery," Liberty Baptist Theological Seminary, September 2008, http://digitalcommons.liberty.edu/cgi/viewcontent.cgi?article=1171&context=doctoral.

6. Proverbs 13:20 ESV

Chapter 8: God Loves My Job More Than Yours

1. Amy L. Sherman, *Kingdom Calling: Vocational Stewardship for the Common Good* (Downers Grove, IL: InterVarsity Press, 2011), 114.

2. Ibid., 115.

3. www.brainyquote.com/quotes/authors/a/abraham_kuyper.html#DLCl2vrKecGoB21s.99.

4. Romans 12:4–5

5. Lucas Kavner, "HuffPost Greatest Person of the Day: Kohl Crecelius Crochets for Communities," *Huffington Post*, May 16, 2011, www.huffingtonpost.com/2011/05/16/huffpost-greatest-person-_n_862542.html.

6. Exodus 35:31–32

7. Os Hillman, "Are We on the Verge of Another Reformation?" *In the Workplace*, www.intheworkplace.com/apps/articles/default.asp?articleid=68281&columnid=1935.

Chapter 9: Worm Food

1. Henri Nouwen, *The Return of the Prodigal Son* (New York: Doubleday, 1992), 40.

2. Brian Osisek, "Aesop's Fables and the Sovereignty of God," *Christian Musings*, March 2, 2012, http://christianmusings-Brian.blogspot.com/2012/03/sovereignty-of-god.html.

3. Rebecca Konyndyk DeYoung, *Glittering Vices: A New Look at the Seven Deadly Sins and Their Remedies* (Grand Rapids, MI: Brazos Press, 2009), 60.

4. Acts 12:23

5. Acts 14:8–17

6. Richard Foster, *The Challenge of the Disciplined Life* (San Francisco: Harper & Row, 1985), 219.

7. François Fénelon, *The Seeking Heart* (Jacksonville, FL: Seedsower Christian Publishing, 1992), 133.

8. Devotional given at the Reynolds Plantation in Georgia, October 21, 2012.

9. Psalm 8:3–4

10. Ken Curtis, PhD, "Bach Created Music to God's Glory," www.christianity.com/church/church-history/timeline/1701-1800/bach-created-music-to-gods-glory-11630186.html.

11. Calvin R. Stapert, "To the Glory of God Alone." *Christianity Today,* 7/01/2007, www.christianitytoday.com/ch/2007/issue95/1.8.html?start=1.

Chapter 10: Panera Prophet

1. 2 Corinthians 12:9–10
2. Proverbs 27:6
3. 1 Samuel 9:2 NLT
4. 1 Samuel 16:12 NIV 1984
5. 1 Samuel 14:47–48
6. Shira Schoenberg, "David—Biblical Jewish King," *Jewish Virtual Library,* www.jewishvirtuallibrary.org/jsource/biography/David.html.
7. 1 Samuel 10:20–22
8. 1 Samuel 16:1–13
9. 1 Samuel 15
10. 2 Samuel 12:13
11. Psalm 51:16–17 THE MESSAGE
12. Heading taken from my friend Mike Foster and the People of the Second Chance.
13. Trisha Davis, "Forgiving the Cheating Pastor," *People of the Second Chance,* August 11, 2012, www.potsc.com/giving-grace/forgiving-the-cheating-pastor-2/.
14. "Our Story," *Refine Us: Restoring Hope, Renewing Relationships,* http://vimeo.com/39354012.
15. Justin Davis, "My Fatal Mistake," Jenni Clayville, August 16, 2010, http://www.jenniclayville.com/justin-davis-my-fatal-mistake/.
16. Justin Davis, "God Isn't Through Yet," *People of the Second Chance,* August 7, 2012, www.potsc.com/giving-grace/inspiration/god-isnt-through-yet/.
17. Psalm 51:4–6 THE MESSAGE

Chapter 11: Who Am I When I'm Not Me?

1. James Mason, "Jesus Loves Me, and That's Enough," *A Chosen Generation,* October 3, 2012, http://jamesmason93.wordpress.com/2012/10/03/jesus-loves-me-and-thats-enough/.

2. Ed Dobson, *Ed's Story,* https://flannel.org/products/eds-story-1-3.

3. Kevin Helliker, "You Might as Well Face It: You're Addicted to Success," *The Wall Street Journal*, February 12, 2009, http://online.wsj.com/article/SB123423234983566171.html.

4. Justin Davis, "What I Wish I Could Tell the 22-Year-Old Me," August 20, 2012, http://refineus.org/2012/08/what-i-wish/.

5. 1 Samuel 22:2 THE MESSAGE

6. 1 Samuel 21:13 THE MESSAGE

7. There is some scholarly debate about whether or not David actually wrote this Psalm, but it is attributed to him at this low point in his life.

8. Psalm 34:8

9. Psalm 34:9

10. *Ed's Story*, https://flannel.org/products/eds-story-1-3.

11. Ibid.

12. Dan Merica, "Facing death, a top pastor rethinks what it means to be Christian," CNN, *CNN Belief Blog*, February 18, 2012, http://religion.blogs.cnn.com/2012/02/18/tending-the-garden-one-person-at-a-time/.

13. Ibid. To see more of Dobson's story see EdsStory.com; "My Garden."

14. Richard Foster, *Prayer: Finding the Heart's True Home* (San Francisco: HarperSanFrancisco, 1992), 7.

Chapter 12: Christian Karma

1. *National and International Service and Mission: Agape Center for Service and Learning Annual Report 2010* (Grantham, PA: Messiah College, Agape Center for Service and Learning, 2010), p. 7, www.messiah.edu/external_programs/agape/annual_reports/documents/NISM.pdf.

2. Psalm 23 NRSV

3. Job 38:3–4 THE MESSAGE

4. *The Catholic Encyclopedia,* "St. Thomas the Apostle," www.newadvent.org/cathen/14658b.htm.

5. Thieleman Van Bragt, *Martyrs' Mirror: The Story of Seventeen Centuries of Christian Martyrdom From the Time of Christ to A.D. 1660,* trans. Joseph E. Sohm (1938), accessed online www.homecomers.org/mirror/martyrs010.htm.

6. The Catholic Encyclopedia, "St. Peter, Prince of the Apostles," www.newadvent.org/cathen/11744a.htm.

7. *The Catholic Encyclopedia,* "St. Andrew," www.newadvent.org/cathen/01471a.htm.

8. John 16:33

9. John Stott, *The Cross of Christ* (Downers Grove, IL: InterVarsity Press, 2006), 326.

10. Ibid., 326–27.

Chapter 13: Spinach Salad With a Side of Shame

1. Matthew 7:3–5 NIV

2. See Luke 7:36–38.

3. Luke 7:44–46

4. Luke 7:47

5. The Gathering, "Opening Session—Social Entrepreneur Spotlight," podcast audio, accessed December 25, 2012, http://thegathering.com/media.html.

Chapter 14: How Do I Look?

1. C. S. Lewis, *Mere Christianity* (New York: HarperCollins, 1952), 125.

2. John 12:43 GW

3. Devotional given at the Reynolds Plantation in Georgia, October 21, 2012.

4. Taken from an introduction of Shane and Shane at The Gathering, September 14, 2012.

5. Brian D. McLaren, "Open Letter to Worship Songwriters (Updated)," *Worship Leader Magazine,* March/April 2005, http://brianmclaren.net/archives/blog/open-letter-to-worship-songwrite.html.

6. Thanks for this insight from my friend Adrianne Thompson.

7. C. S. Lewis, *Mere Christianity* (New York: HarperCollins, 2001), 123.

8. Tim Keller, *The Freedom of Self-Forgetfulness* (Leyland, England: 10Publishing, 2012), Kindle, chapter 2, paragraph 3.

9. 1 Corinthians 4:3–4

10. 1 Timothy 1:15

11. Tim Keller, *The Freedom of Self-Forgetfulness,* Kindle, chapter 3, paragraph 1.

12. Ibid., Kindle, chapter 2, paragraph 9.

Chapter 15: A Full Head and an Empty Heart

1. Ezra 7:10

2. Matthew 3:7

3. Matthew 23:27

4. Matthew 23:33

5. Luke 11:46

6. Ray Hollenbach "Jesus the Know-It-All," Churchleaders.com, www
.churchleaders.com/pastors/pastor-how-to/152916-ray-hollenbach-jesus
-the-know-it-all.html.

7. "The Heart of Paul's Theology: Paul and the Corinthians," http://
elearning.thirdmill.org/theme/standard_thirdmill/lessons/hpt4text.html.

8. 1 Corinthians 1:27–29

Chapter 16: Man Makeup

1. Matthew 23:27

2. Revelation 3:16

3. Personal conversation at the Reynolds Plantation in Georgia, October 21, 2012.

4. Psalm 139:23–24

5. Revelation 3:20

Chapter 17: You-Turn

1. Philippians 3:8 THE MESSAGE

2. 1 Timothy 1:15

3. 1 Corinthians 9:27

4. Dallas Willard, *Spirit of the Disciplines* (New York: HarperCollins, 1991), 4–5.

5. Proverbs 4:23 NIV 1984

6. 2 Corinthians 12:9

7. Elvina M. Hall, "Jesus Paid It All," 1865, public domain.

8. Romans 7:25

9. Tim Keller, Twitter post, September 9, 2012, 5:03 a.m., https://twitter
.com/DailyKeller/status/244767896914497538.

10. Luke 7:47

11. Ed Reese, "The Life and Ministry of James Hudson Taylor," *Wholesome Words,* www.wholesomewords.org/missions/biotaylor2.html.

12. Dr. and Mrs. Howard Taylor, *J. Hudson's Taylor's Spiritual Secret* (Chicago: Moody Publishers, 2009), 163.

13. Ibid.

14. "Biography of J. Hudson Taylor," *Christian Classics Ethereal Library,* http://www.ccel.org/ccel/taylor_jh.

15. Ed Reese, "The Life and Ministry of James Hudson Taylor."

16. Dr. and Mrs. Howard Taylor, *J. Hudson Taylor's Spiritual Secret,* 240.

17. Louisa Lim, "In The Land Of Mao, A Rising Tide Of Christianity," NPR, July 19, 2010, http://www.npr.org/2010/07/19/128546334/in-the-land-of-mao-a-rising-tide-of-christianity.

Conclusion

1. Mark 7:21, italics mine

ACKNOWLEDGMENTS

This book is a collective project and simply would not have been possible without a team of supportive family and friends. Special thanks to:

Laurel, my amazing wife. You have been ridiculously encouraging of my work. Thank you for saying "yes" on a rooftop in Kigali and for always telling me when I have spinach in my teeth.

Anna Haggard. You have a gift in writing and joyfully worked tirelessly on this project. Without question, this book would not have happened without you.

Allie Speck. You were so much more than "just a research intern." You significantly shaped the content of this book and showed us how to live a life of courageous hope.

Andrew Wolgemuth. You are so very good at what you do, and it's a privilege to have you as my agent and my friend.

Andy McGuire, Ellen Chalifoux, Brett Benson, Carra Carr, and the rest of the outstanding team at Bethany House. I could not imagine having a more positive experience with a publisher. Every step of the writing process, you exceeded our expectations.

Brian Fikkert. Thank you for being willing to write the foreword, for your tremendous friendship, and for modeling the right way to do good.

HOPE Staff. From Jeff Brown's suggestions on the cover to Kevin Tordoff's creative marketing skills to Nick Martino's support in coordinating so many logistics, I have a team of incredible colleagues who supported this project and constantly go above and beyond. Working together with you is a privilege.

Angela Scheff and Phil Smith. Thank you for helping me discover my love of writing.

Tim Keller. Thank you for modeling Christ-centered leadership and for your teaching that has influenced so many of the themes of this book.

Family. Jon, Jen, Amy, Ryan, Heather, Paul, Kelly, Brent, Ashley, Nana, Gramps, Mom, and Dad. Thank you for shaping who I am and providing a loving family as the background to this book. Jon, a special thanks to you for making time to give your feedback during your relocation to Grand Rapids.

Friends who generously allowed me to share their stories. A very special thank you to Sparky and Carrie Grace, Justin and Trisha Davis, Alan and Katherine Barnhart, Kevin and Lynn Yan, Greg Lafferty, Courtney Rountree Mills, Jon Tyson, Kurt Keilhacker, Scott Harrison, Ryan O'Neal, Eric and Pennie Thurman, Beth Birmingham, Billy Nolan, Jeff and Sue Rutt, Kohl Crecelius, Jenn Moody, Jean Marie Musangwa, Dennis Hollinger, and Mike Foster.

My Houston Friends. Thank you for modeling real friendship. Special thanks to David Weekley, Rusty Walter, Terry Looper, John Montgomery, Tiger Dawson, Wil Van Loh, and Kevin Hunt.

My 3 a.m. friends, especially Jon Greer, Baxter Underwood, David Norman, Chris Martin, and my Kelly B303 roommates.

Carolyn Haggard and the talented team at RainCloud Media. Thank you for expertly helping to share these stories.

Friends who generously reviewed this manuscript and made massive improvements, including Chris Horst, Fred Smith, Jonathan Merritt, Matthew Anderson, Ken Uhrich, Phil Smith, Bill Gaultiere, Lance Wood, Brian Lewis, Alison McLennan, Todd Hendricks, David Spickard, Madelyn Houser, Katie Nienow, Adrianne Thompson, Don Eberly, Chris Heuertz, Maggie and Jean-Louis Kali, Josh Kwan, Ray Chung, the Haggard family, Bobby Parschauer, Meggie Monahan, Erin Longenecker, Jeff Shinabarger, Jim Deitch, Adrianne Thompson, and Cathi Linch.

My Savior. It is your grace I want to reflect and live out. May your power be made perfect in my weakness.

Peter Greer is a follower of Jesus, advocate for the poor, author, and president and CEO of HOPE International, a global faith-based microenterprise development organization serving entrepreneurs throughout Africa, Asia, Latin America, and Eastern Europe. Peter and his wife, Laurel, have three children and live in Lancaster, Pennsylvania.

Peter is a graduate of Messiah College (BS, 1997), Harvard University's Kennedy School of Government (MPP, 2004) and Erskine College (honorary PhD, 2012).

Peter served as a microfinance adviser in Phnom Penh, Cambodia. He also served as a technical adviser for Self-Help Development Foundation (CARE Zimbabwe) in Bulawayo, Zimbabwe. In 1999, he became the managing director for URWEGO Community Bank in Kigali, Rwanda.

As an advocate for the church's role in missions and ending extreme poverty, Greer has been a featured speaker at leading conferences such as Harvard's International Development Conference, Catalyst, Urbana, Passion, and Jubilee.

Peter co-authored a faith-based book on microfinance, *The Poor Will Be Glad* (Zondervan, 2009) and co-authored a children's book on international adoption, *Mommy's Heart Went POP!* (Russell Media, 2012). He is working on his next book, *Mission Drift* (Bethany House, 2014).

Follow Peter on twitter: @peterkgreer.

To contact Peter for a speaking engagement, please visit www.peterkgreer.com.

Anna Haggard is the executive writing assistant at HOPE International, where she collaborates with the president and the marketing department to share HOPE's message through print and social media. Anna is a graduate of Asbury University and lives in Lancaster, Pennsylvania.

Get an Inside Look at the Specific Challenges and Spiritual Dangers Facing Christian Organizations

As Christian organizations grow, the Gospel often becomes cursory, expendable, or even forgotten. Again and again, leaders have watched their ministries, businesses, and nonprofits professionalize, expand, and lose sight of their original goals. Even churches can stray from their calling.

Mission Drift provides the tools leaders need to keep their organizations "mission true" or get back on track. Supported by research and filled with compelling anecdotes, *Mission Drift* identifies organizations that exhibit intentional, long-term commitment to Christ in contrast to those that have wandered away from their core beliefs.

All leaders will face mission drift at some point. Peter Greer and Chris Horst show readers how to leave an enduring Christian legacy rather than drifting off course.

Mission Drift by Peter Greer and Chris Horst
AVAILABLE FEBRUARY 2014